D1565029

THE MAVERICK EXECUTIVE

THE MAVERICK EXECUTIVE

Robert N. McMurry

amacom

A Division Of American Management Associations

Library of Congress Cataloging in Publication Data

McMurry, Robert N
     The maverick executive.

     1. Executives. 2. Management. 3. Leadership.
I. Title.
HF5500.2.M225   658.4   73-85189
ISBN 0-8144-5345-7

© 1974 AMACOM
A division of American Management Associations, New York.
All rights reserved. Printed in the United States of America.

International standard book number: 0-8144-5345-7
Library of Congress catalog card number: 73-85189

First printing

TO MY WIFE

Preface

In this book I have chosen to portray an extremely rare type of executive whose extraordinary capacities, qualities, and skills have been virtually unrecognized in management literature. Despite this oversight, the Maverick Executive is not a freak or a curiosity; the accomplishments of this type have been spectacular in providing the initiative and drive that not only produce successful "growth" companies but also can salvage those that are faltering.

The portrait of the Maverick Executive presented here is not a theoretical concept; it has been built empirically, inductively, on the basis of the observation of many executives in action. This has been supplemented by interviews with several thousand candidates for executive positions and by close and continuing relationships with dozens of senior executives.

There is no doubt that the Maverick Executive deserves to be carefully studied on the basis of performance alone. However, in developing this portrait it became increasingly clear to me that the strengths and weaknesses of this type of executive expose and clarify in many notable ways the strengths and weaknesses I have found in orthodox executives during my forty years of working with the people problems of management. Indeed, the Maverick Executive's unconventional characteristics corroborate, in many respects, what I have found to be invariably true: business is an Alice-in-Wonderland world where few things are quite what they are purported to be. And the phenomenon of the Maverick Executive demonstrates how filled the business world is with tough realities, challenges, illusions, unbelievable blunders, and blind spots.

By looking closely at the Maverick Executive it is possible to see a great deal that has escaped the notice not only of students and theorists of management but of many executives as well. For example, of all the people problems facing management, those arising from overdependence are, in my observation, the most serious. This condition, as I see it, is the greatest contributor to job failure in industry, whether it be in sales, supervision, or any other level of management. It is therefore to be especially noted that the Maverick Executive is preeminently free from this malady of overdependence. At the same time, however, the Maverick's style of management, which is common to many other executives, is one that most satisfies the dependency needs of subordinates.

Similarly, a great many executives share many of the Maverick Executive's naive beliefs about people and their problems. These common errors of managerial comprehension range from ignorance about human values and communications to ignorance about the assessment, training, and placement of personnel, and the salvaging of those who have reached their first level of incompetence. Yet very few executives have the Maverick Executive's skills in leadership and the acquisition of power.

All that I have discovered to be true of the Maverick Executive solidly supports my own convictions about people in business. Like this type of executive, I question the belief that people are naturally good, rational, and logical and can be constructively influenced by information and training. Therefore I also agree with the judgment of the Maverick Executive that management development programs are largely a waste of time. I do accept that employees can acquire skills and that their attitudes and values can be changed, but not by direct, logical confrontation or formal training or admonition.

Furthermore, I hold, as does the Maverick Executive, that the great majority (roughly three fourths) of all employees are inherently fearful and immature and, like children, tend to be selfish and demanding. As a psychologist, I would call them inherently anxious and overdependent, with strong needs for security and the support of strong leaders. Like the Maverick Executive, I have long since accepted the fact that many employees regard their jobs with attitudes ranging from mild tolerance to acute distaste, and that very few jobs can be enriched to provide challenge, excitement, and opportunity.

I am also as skeptical as any Maverick Executive about the panaceas that have been successively offered to solve management's problems. Such programs often seem plausible, attract wide attention and many followers, and then they fade away. In my experience no plan, program, or technique has yet been developed which has more than a partial, transient, or incidental effect in coping with the more serious people problems facing industry. For practical purposes, as the case of the Maverick Executive makes clear, the chief executive today is no better equipped than he was five decades ago.

These observations—inevitably somewhat cynical— are primarily the result of my forty years of actual working experience in business. For my professional qualifications alone (I hold advanced degrees in psychology from the Universities of Chicago and Vienna and am a member of the Chicago Psychoanalytical Society) would not have enabled me to recognize the truly significant behaviors of executives and their subordinates. I have been an office boy in the Chicago stockyards, a cab driver, an hourly worker in a factory, a door-to-door salesman of vacuum cleaners, a supervisor and manager, an entrepreneur, an executive, and a management consultant. I have built a consulting organization now widely known in the personnel field; I have been an expert witness in class action cases and have successfully countered union organizing drives; I have sat at the bargaining table in union negotiations and have worked closely as an adviser to top executives on a wide variety of people problems in enterprises of all sizes and kinds in the United States and abroad.

Through such experiences I have learned, at first hand, a great deal that is not found in the management textbooks. And I have seen management's problems compounded again and again by theories and advice from all kinds of behavioral scientists. It is therefore my hope that this study of the Maverick Executive will help to provide a kind of bridge of realism between the contributions of the psychological laboratory and clinic and the real-life problems of the subculture that industry is. As a potent and unique element of that subculture, the Maverick Executive is certainly not the ideal executive, but he has strengths that provide realistic answers to some of the toughest people problems in industry. And he has weaknesses that point up what every executive has to overcome in order to meet the full responsibility of management.

Robert N. McMurry

Contents

WHAT IS A
MAVERICK EXECUTIVE?

1

In the spring of 1973, the General Motors Corporation announced the resignation of 48-year-old John Z. DeLorean, who had been vice president and group executive of all GM car and truck divisions. He had had a brilliant career with GM, was earning $550,000 a year, and was very likely to become the president of the corporation. His resignation astonished the automobile industry as well as outsiders. But John DeLorean had his own very specific reasons for dropping out of GM, and one of them shortly became the title of a *Fortune* article about him: "The Automobile Industry Has Lost Its Masculinity." [1]

Among the other reasons cited for DeLorean's departure were GM's policies on marketing small cars and on emission standards; its bureaucratization and isolation from competitive realities; its executive committee meetings with limited alternatives for planning or modifying proposals; and government regulations.

[1] *Fortune*, September 1973.

DeLorean told *Fortune* editor Rush Loving, "It was like standing in the boiler room and tending a machine and you were just watching it instead of running it." And so he left. He became president of the National Alliance for Businessmen, which helps find jobs for disadvantaged minorities, but eventually he aims to do what he is most eminently capable of doing: "I'm best at taking a weak business and making it strong. That's a unique gift. There aren't too many guys who do that."

In these words DeLorean concisely describes the major forte of that extraordinary combination of capacities, talents, qualities, attitudes, and behaviors which I call the Maverick Executive. And according to published reports, DeLorean seems to have most of the qualifications of such an executive. *The New York Times* called him "The General Motors Maverick," but his words and actions indicate he is much more than an executive who does not conform to the GM pattern. He would not conform to any corporation's executive pattern. On the basis of what his interviewers have reported, he is abrasive, idealistic, nonconformist, driving, tyrannical, creative, insubordinate, hero-worshipping, perfectionistic, innovative, inspiring, moralistic, individualistic.

In short, DeLorean greatly resembles the kind of executive described in this book. It is the kind that undoubtedly annoys or infuriates many of the men now running U.S. corporations. Even those who might consider hiring or promoting a Maverick Executive would be very unlikely to choose such a man to succeed themselves. His kind is not considered sufficiently conformist and "safe." All too often he has "dangerous" thoughts. Yet in my judgment the Maverick Executive is potentially the most effective and valuable executive to be found in any organization, and in a growing company he can be worth more than all the orthodox members of management put together.

Many successful executives exhibit many of the Maverick Executive's characteristics, but he definitely is not to be confused with many nonconformist mavericks in management, those eccentric, recalcitrant businessmen who are usually rebels without a cause. Some of these men are highly publicized, especially when their tactics are either flamboyant or manipulative. Others of this type are known and resented only by close colleagues inside their organizations. Such businessmen are mavericks, to be sure, but they are not maverick *executives*. They are posturing egocentrics who flout the most basic rules of management and executive behavior. They have no true leadership qualities and no desire to learn the techniques and strategies that might even make them good managers; in fact, they are hacks at management. For the most part they are anxious and obsessed with the trappings of power, like the company president who had his company procure white Cadillacs for the members of his executive staff and then each noon led them in a garish procession to dine at his favorite restaurant.

The kind of executive we are concerned with is a very different sort of maverick. His greatest single distinctive asset as an executive is his freedom from anxiety and the problems arising from it. In my obser-

vations I have found that at least *three fourths* of the
Maverick Executive's contemporaries in all levels of
management suffer from outright and often paralyz-
ing anxiety. A similar prevalence of anxiety in the
American culture has been suggested by the findings
of a study made by the U.S. Department of Health,
Education and Welfare's Public Health Service: 58
percent of a nationwide sample of 6,672 civilians between the ages of 18 and 79 reported "nervousness"
as one of their symptoms, and an additional 17 percent
said they had either had a nervous breakdown or felt
one impending.[2] Thus 75 percent of this sample may
be said to suffer significantly from anxiety, since this
condition is one of the principal components of "nervousness" which is most invariably characteristic of
nervous breakdowns. The Maverick Executive is totally free of "nervousness"; he can make very threatening decisions with equanimity because of his healthy
ego and tremendous self-confidence and optimism.

However, what distinguishes the Maverick Executive from *all* other executives is his[3] rare constellation of characteristics, skills, attitudes, strengths, and
weaknesses. His most notable marks are his exceptional drive, courage, optimism, and decisiveness. But
a listing of his features would also embrace an extraordinary diversity of terms, many paradoxical: excitable

[2] *Selected Symptoms of Psychological Distress* (Public
Health Service Publication No. 1000, Series 11, No. 37,
August 1970).

[3] The male personal pronoun is not used here thoughtlessly.
I have never heard of or observed a female Maverick Executive.

and tireless, self-confident and intolerant, suspicious and gullible, decisive and nonanalytical, dedicated and fickle, innovative and conservative, superficial and profound, persevering and nonconforming, autocratic and versatile, inspiring and ruthless, indifferent and meddling, impetuous and rigid, obsessive and careless, scheming and unreflective, demanding and casual, critical and idolizing.

Many executives exhibit some of these attributes, but very few have them in combination and to the extent—and have the freedom to exercise them—of the Maverick Executive. A very significant difference is that his qualities of drive and decisiveness are heightened in every way; in these two respects he surpasses all his colleagues. And his whole complex mix of traits and attributes is an unusual alloy of inherent strengths and weaknesses that has been toughened and sharpened by hard experience in the business world. *Physiologically* the Maverick Executive is healthy and robust (rarely have I seen one who is an ectomorph, thin and delicate) and he seems to be constantly flooded with adrenalin, so tremendous is his energy and drive. *Psychologically* he has the makeup of a person whom psychiatrists often characterize as mildly hypomanic or hyperkinetic.

However, he is no way mentally ill; indeed his self-confidence and optimism are unfailing, and his goal is always to win. He tends to be constantly stimulated and his tempo is always accelerated. He has great capacity for overwork and quick recovery. This particular personality syndrome is also exhibited by many of the best salesmen.

7

But the Maverick Executive, because he is hyper-kinetic, also has many weaknesses. For example, his tendency to become overenthusiastic can lead him into questionable projects, and his tendency to overconfidence can make him reluctant to listen to advice and impatient with detail. He may make decisions impulsively and because of his accelerated operating tempo he may be superficial in analyzing problems.

His impersonal attitudes toward his subordinates are also notable. He has learned never to trust even his closest subordinates, for he knows they are not as dedicated to his goals as he is. Yet he is adept at motivating his subordinates by appealing to their self-interest and exploiting their desire to be led. He has, however, no illusions about employees in general—in his opinion, most of them are passive, dependent, anxious, insecure, and submissive. Having these attitudes, the Maverick Executive is insensitive to others, intolerant of their failings, and usually oblivious of their feelings; he is, therefore, rarely close to people and is a poor communicator.

Nevertheless, the Maverick Executive has so many superior qualities and abilities that his weaknesses are more than counterbalanced. His drive, his optimism, his decisiveness, his readiness to take risks, are *real*, not compensatory. Characteristics that might be considered faults according to currently acceptable criteria are, in fact, among his superlative virtues. His willingness to take risks, which makes him difficult to predict and sometimes a little dangerous, is the *sine qua non* of his success; indeed, his courage to make hard, ruthless decisions, to upset and reorder things, will often make a company grow even if the industry as a whole is lagging.

Inevitably, his lack of docility and his nonconformity make the Maverick Executive very unpopular in many industries—in banking, insurance, and railroading, for example—and especially unwelcome in governmental and military bureaucracies. In these environments he often becomes so threatening to the established, rigid hierarchies (and particularly to his superiors) that he is feared, opposed, and sabotaged when possible. Even in a very large, progressive organization, such as an IBM or a General Electric, the Maverick Executive may find the going extremely tough before he manages to reach the top echelons of power where his capacities can have the scope they need to function.

The Maverick Executive has been largely ignored in the literature of management, especially by behavioral scientists. This is because he has not been previously identified as a type, *sui generis*, and because his often abrasive tactics are disliked by those who have been beguiled by the panaceas of permissive, participative management and collaborative decision making by committees. Yet in the light of the illusions, the rigid value systems, and the traditional mores of the hard-nosed leaders who are responsible for corporate performance, the Maverick Executive's behavior is much more thoroughly in accord with the tough realities of the world of business than is that of the so-called democratic executives. The greatest builders of American businesses—the McCormicks, the Fords, the Rockefellers—have always been nonconformists, innovators whose behavior made them mavericks in the eyes of their contemporaries. Furthermore, all of them were autocratic to some degree; most were abrasive and none practiced democratic-participative management.

Certainly the Maverick Executive bears little resemblance to the old stereotype of a successful executive, the man in the gray flannel suit: a hard-hitting, gregarious manager who is expert at all jobs, suave, well-groomed, considerate to employees, emotionally balanced, and a keen judge of people. This image simply does not square with reality. However, the more sophisticated images that are advanced by many students of management are just as illusory. Such observers commonly associate the successful executive with certain theoretical behaviors and capacities: he is a good administrator, he aims for efficiency, promotes management development and participative management, he is intent on problem solving, increasing profits, and establishing a good earnings and operations record. This is the prototype of the *middle manager*, not of the chief executive who is growth oriented. Likewise, such terms do not apply to the Maverick Executive.

I have observed and evaluated hundreds of senior and junior executives, including the unsuccessful, the apparently successful, and the outstandingly successful. Viewed superficially, these three kinds of executives show no significant differences in makeup. On the other hand, when the executive is studied in depth, in spite of the variegated pattern of his day-to-day behavior, the Maverick emerges unmistakably. To

10

sharpen the portrait, let us contrast what he *is* with what he is *not:*

—He is not one to run scared. His courage to risk failure without anxiety is his most distinctive characteristic. He is ready to risk losing his job or even compromising his security and future in order to gain his goals.

—He never strolls but always runs; he overworks himself and recovers quickly. His motor never runs down. His boundless energy often leads him to expect more of his subordinates than they can accomplish for him.

—He does not feel inferior to anyone, nor is he neurotically compelled to compete with anyone. His unfailing, sometimes exaggerated, self-confidence enables him to make even the hardest decisions on his own. He is strongly inner-directed.

—He is not modest concerning his abilities. He has a large but healthy ego and a realistic estimate of his capacities.

—He is neither reserved nor cautious, but is continually enthusiastic about what he is doing. Like the supersalesman and the evangelist, he is genuinely sold on himself and on the importance of his work.

—He is rarely worried and never anxious. He is overoptimistic and can become oversold on a project or an idea. Fascination with mergers, for example, may make him "conglomerate-crazy."

—He is not very analytical and often relies on hunches or intuition, which can lead him to some superficial conclusions. Because his evaluations are

11

based on impressions and appearances, he is a poor judge of people.

—He is not inclined to be orderly, but does carefully structure the functions of his subordinates. He does not bother very much about detail in establishing the ways and means used to organize and maintain things.

—He is not good at maintaining the status quo of a going business. He is superb at initiating and building up a new business or revitalizing one that is on the downgrade.

—He is not flexible about his values. He holds adamantly to the work ethic—hard work, perseverance, respect for authority. He is so steeped in this ethic that he finds it virtually impossible to change his attitude when he is challenged, for example, by a young manager who resents authority and wants to take it into his own hands despite his inexperience.

—He is not a conventional planner. One of his greatest contributions to management is his intuitive ability to identify and understand opportunities and relationships that go unnoticed by his colleagues or competitors. He sees new applications of old ideas, and he senses subtle implications having far-reaching economic consequences for his company. He has serendipity.

—He is not patient. His need to achieve drives him mercilessly toward the goals he sets for himself. His methods are totally realistic, not always "nice," and he does not hesitate to take an expedient course or to be ruthless when necessary, so that he occasionally accomplishes what others regard as impossible.

—He is not an administrator in the conventional sense. He is the dominant strategist who sets goals and priorities of all programs, rarely delegates ultimate authority to others, and centralizes control of the organization in his hands.

—He purposefully avoids introspection and does not examine himself subjectively. Thus he has poor or superficial perceptions of himself and his failings.

—He is not naive about the demands of rulership. A master of corporate politics, he manipulates others to gain and hold the power he must have in order to lead. He is skilled in strategies that win the support of his superiors and his peers, and is especially expert in impressing dominant directors, stockholders, and other influential persons not only in industry and government, but in his community and, sometimes, labor leaders as well.

—He is not a disciple of participative management. He makes all major and many minor decisions. He may be intellectually aware of other styles of management, but his one and only style is that of a benevolent autocrat.

—He is not a permissive or lenient ruler, and he can be ruthless. He is a tremendously magnetic, natural leader who leads by influence, not command. He knows that to rule effectively he must convince subordinates that he knows exactly what he is doing and that he has their interests at heart, even though it may not be in accord with what they want or think is right.

—He is not softhearted about employees and has little empathy or real concern for others. He is convinced that most subordinates are passive, insecure, dependent, and intellectually rigid. He is usually blind to their individual differences and intolerant of their failings when dealing with them personally.

—He is not interested in management development because he has learned management predominantly by trial and error and not in schools, and he has found that most people have limited management potential. He is aware of two broad classes of personnel—the self-reliant and the dependent—and is unaware of the different demands of the various classes of employees he is actually managing.

—He cannot tolerate strong, independent subordinates and he has no interest in, or capacity for, finding a successor for himself, although he may give the concept lip service.

—He is not a fraternizer. He tends to isolate himself, carefully keeping his distance from those under him.

—He does not concentrate on operating efficiency or solving minor problems. He is an entrepreneur of sorts whose imagination and initiative drive him to seek opportunities and take risks that will keep his company growing ahead of its competitors. He recognizes that what his company is doing currently, no matter how successful, is to some degree obsolete. He is constantly running to keep in place.

—He is no world-saving humanitarian or idealist in any utopian sense. An earthy pragmatist, he is keenly concerned with successful performance and profits; but he has acquired the ideals of men he admires as heroes and he usually cherishes some goal beyond the economic. He has a sense of mission in driving to reach it.

From the foregoing, it should be apparent why the Maverick Executive is a rarity, so much so, that perhaps not one in a thousand of all the chief executives now managing corporations would closely fit his description. This is partly because he is usually kept out of the top post by those who are in a position to promote him but who cannot tolerate his ways. Once in power, however, he soon demonstrates his capacity for leadership. He shows his subordinates that he can accomplish, often at great effort, what he has decided should be accomplished. He decides on changes in direction, assumes great risks in innovations, struggles against overwhelming odds, and so forcefully impresses his subordinates that they view him as a model and enthusiastically follow his lead. The loyalty his kind of leadership invokes in a subordinate is like that of a disciple, a true believer.

With this kind of industrial leadership, the Maverick Executive achieves his ultimate stature by *influencing* others, not by commanding them. Conventional executives (especially the insecure), who must rely largely on titles and the other trappings of authority to insure their subordinates' conformity to their orders, are never able to achieve this kind of leadership. But this is a role for which the Maverick Executive is particularly fitted because of his charisma, personal magnetism, drive, and infectious enthusiasm. These are the by-products of behavior that lead people to admire, trust, and respect such an executive so much that they will seek to emulate him. These capacities give him the stature not only to gain and hold the power he needs to implement his decisions, but to motivate his subordinates to follow his leadership willingly, even eagerly.

How did the Maverick Executive get to be what he is? To begin with, he was born with better equipment. He is endowed with a hormonal constitution that insures his energy, self-reliance, and optimism. In addition, he has a very sturdy constitution and excellent health, without which he could never withstand the pressures and stresses to which his drives subject him in his executive career. Even when he does contract some illness, his physical resistance is so high that he can usually continue to operate almost as though he were unaffected.

With this basis of a cast-iron constitution and a hypomanic physical (hormonal) endowment, the Maverick Executive develops a personality marked by obsessive drives, which, should he engage in business, are subsequently directed toward the acquisition of power, recognition, and money. (Others of this breed may seek political power or religious leadership.) These tendencies have been conditioned, usually, by his early environment, which is most often middle class. Invariably he has at least one driving parent whom he admired, frequently his mother.

Typically, he has had heroes (usually successful entrepreneurs) whom he respected and admired. As he tried to emulate the particular people in his environment whom he admired, he developed habits, values, and goals that stimulated him to seek success as a manager. Habits of industry, perseverance, and decisiveness have come to be so firmly conditioned in him that they are essentially reflex. This syndrome, superimposed on a foundation of health, drive, inherent self-confidence, and optimism, makes success almost inevitable.

During his childhood and youth, a Maverick Executive has usually had the opportunity to exercise and mature his values and capacities in an environment where he can perfect his skills. Adverse circumstances slow down his development, but they do not impede it. However, much depends on his being in the right place at the right time. He may become the protégé of his employer, or of someone else whose reputation and advice help him develop his innate talents.

Formal education and training for the Maverick Executive are almost incidental. He learns principally through experience, through trial and error; formal management training simply sharpens and amplifies his skills, techniques, and business judgments. Many of the most successful Maverick Executives never went to college; few known to me ever acquired an M.B.A. Lack of formal education, of course, sometimes distorts the Maverick's thinking. One in particular, who built a very successful manufacturing business, was so sensitive about his not having a college degree that he would not hire anyone who did. He preferred, as he put it, to take only graduates of "the college of hard knocks." His policy may have lost for the company several potentially excellent executives, but, being a Maverick Executive, he was not looking for strong subordinates who might challenge his leadership.

The Maverick Executive's talents for self-propulsion quickly evidence themselves when he becomes a manager and starts his climb up the corporate ladder. He does not tarry, and that is why he is practically never found among those loyal, long-service managers who labor cautiously in the ranks of middle management. He has too much upward mobility. If his drive to reach the top of the organization does not carry him up fast enough, if he is blocked by an imbedded senior executive or by nepotism or by antipathy from someone at the top, he either moves out of the company or he maneuvers sideways to get around the impediment on his way to the top job. For he knows that that is the only place where his talents can flower.

HOW HE DIFFERS FROM OTHER CHIEF EXECUTIVES

2

Care must be taken to distinguish the Maverick Executive from another type commonly found in management, the *overstriver*, who is often a paranoid personality. He too is compulsively ambitious and has a tremendous drive to win high office, prestige, and recognition. But in most other respects he differs widely. Dr. Willard Gaylin, clinical professor of psychiatry at Columbia University's medical school, has well described the dangers of this type:

> The paranoid personality, with his conspiratorial mind, his tendency to personalize, his readiness to see policy challenges as personal attacks, his preoccupation with pride and humiliation, his endless tendency to create power struggles where none need to exist, his constant reassertion of his courage which is not being questioned and his masculinity which is not being threatened, his exaggerated sense of humiliation and his terror of exposing his deeply

felt sense of impotence and inadequacy, is a particular threat in a position of power.[1]

Unfortunately, as Dr. Gaylin points out, these sociopathic traits make a man well suited for gaining power in competitive societies. Moreover, the manifest traits of the overstriver—self-confidence, overemphasis on masculinity, driving ambition—are considered by most people, including executives and corporate directors, to be the marks of a strong leader. Yet the overstriver's drive is neurotic, and so is his artificial or compensatory self-confidence. He wears a mask to conceal his true feelings of inadequacy, which often include a well-developed but hidden hostility.

The difference between the overstriving entrepreneur and the Maverick Executive can be seen most clearly in the area of egotism. Underlying both these types—in fact, all hard-driving executives—is a powerful ego; indeed, egotism is the critical source of their success and its expression takes many forms. As Antony Jay has pointed out,[2] there is a typical cluster of specific traits in the entrepreneurial figure: egotism, vanity, selfishness, desire for recognition, and speed at taking offense. All these are manifestations of strong ego feeling, which may have psychological variations. In the overstriver this egotism is usually compensa-

[1] Willard Gaylin, "In Matters Mental or Emotional, What's Normal?" *The New York Times Magazine*, April 1, 1973.
[2] Antony Jay, *Management and Machiavelli* (New York: Holt, Rinehart & Winston, 1968), p. 133.

tory, a reaction to a strong conviction that he is edu-
cationally, socially, or intellectually inadequate. Or
his egotism may express his reaction to rejection by
his parents, by WASPs, or by other admired figures.

Because of such reactions, much of the egotism of
many great entrepreneurs is fueled by resentment and
dislike. These overstriving entrepreneurial leaders, as
Jay makes clear, often have strong persecution complexes; they regard those who are not wholly their
friends as their enemies, motivated by personal ani-
mosity and conspiratorially united against them. They
love and hate more strongly than other people do.
Their hostilities are often turned inward, which stimulates them to engage in self-punitive acts—as Jay puts
it, "to scorn delights and live laborious days."

In these respects, the overstriver exhibits symptoms
of what psychoanalyst Karen Horney has defined as
"basic anxiety," a feeling of isolation, helplessness, and
profound insecurity produced by experiences that
have made the individual fearful of a world he sees
as potentially hostile.[3] Horney found such anxiety to
be so characteristic of Western competitive culture
that it was responsible for "the neurotic personality
of our time." She found that neurotic people developed three ways of coping with their basic anxiety—
by rebelling and fighting others, by clinging to
stronger people, or by emotionally withdrawing from
others. Lacking self-confidence and feeling isolated
and hostile, the insecure anxious person feels com-

[3] Karen Horney, *Neurosis and Human Growth* (New York:
W. W. Norton, 1950), pp. 18–25.

pelled to lift himself above others and to develop an idealized image of himself, which he gradually identifies as his idealized self. This process of self-glorification impels him to prove himself in action in a series of drives that Horney calls "the search for glory." Because of its compensatory nature, this search impels him to strive for perfection, to excel in everything, and to achieve a "vindictive triumph" by humiliating, defeating, or frustrating others through gaining success and power.

Neurotic ambition and vindictiveness are highly visible in the overstriver, but the drives of the Maverick Executive do not exhibit the neurotic tendencies described by Horney. This is because he is free from anxiety, a fact that is fundamentally his greatest asset. In this respect he differs not only from the overstriver but also from the great majority of his colleagues in management and of all other employees. Anxious people in the working population have acute needs for structure, guidance, and support. They often find themselves over their heads in their jobs because they cannot make the decisions required of them; frequently, they develop psychogenic disorders such as ulcers, hypertension, colitis, and alcoholism. For such people, the most acceptable kind of supervision is benevolent autocracy, which is the very kind that a Maverick Executive employs.

The Maverick Executive's behavior is also markedly different from that of the many great autocratic leaders and entrepreneurs who have been dominant figures in industry, politics, and the arts and sciences. His ego, like theirs, is large but it is reasonably healthy, and although he may be easily wounded by criticism, he has not developed a persecution complex. He is not unduly sensitive to others, nor is he touchy about his own achievements or lack of them. He does not develop hostility toward real or supposed rivals and enemies; in his self-confidence, he is above personal animosities. While the overstriver may be consumed with greed for power or money in his "search for glory," the Maverick Executive is impelled primarily by his delight with challenges, by his sense of mission, and by his dedication to his objectives.

It is these qualities that give the Maverick Executive much of his charisma and magnetism. The combination of his dedication, enthusiasm, his need to search for challenge and strive toward objectives that his subordinates consider worthwhile, evokes an enthusiastic and loyal response from them. He makes them feel that their own work is worthy. Because his standards are consonant with theirs, he confirms and endorses their values, thus reenforcing their identification with him.

At the same time, paradoxically, the Maverick gratifies the masochistic needs of his subordinates. They are never sure that he wholly accepts them; there is always the suspicion that he might replace them or ignore their needs should he decide this is necessary to the attainment of his objectives. In his total dedication to his cause, the Maverick Executive expects his subordinates to be equally identified with it and to be willing to make corresponding sacrifices for it. Those who do not feel such identification or willingness regard him as a harsh taskmaster. One very successful

Maverick Executive went so far as to identify his enterprise with God's work, and anyone on his staff who did not do his utmost was considered not only a disloyal employee but an unbeliever.

Even though the Maverick Executive is not moved by empathy, his sensitivity to things and events is far greater than that of the conventional executive and equal to that of the best entrepreneur. He has exquisitely sensitive antennae, which are always tuned to the world about him and to which he is ever responsive. They provide him with constant feedback on what is happening in his organization and they warn him of problems. He picks up signals that may be very faint to others—an expression on a subordinate's face, a tone of voice, some bit of information overheard in a conversation, an odd statistic in the financial statement, a small change in some routine, or the absence of someone at a particular meeting. He takes notice of slight intimations of trouble and explores them thoroughly.

It is not to be assumed that hyperperceptiveness is a part of every chief executive's sensitive ego. It seems logical that because a chief executive is the one to be most affected when something goes wrong in his organization he will be the one most receptive to the warning signals. In many cases, however, his awareness is seriously distorted, if not totally blocked, by the interference of the immediate subordinates upon whom he depends to keep him informed. The Maverick Executive, since he trusts no one completely, allows no such distortions, and his perceptivity is sharpened acutely by his quick intelligence in recognizing possible trouble. He has a sixth sense about what is important and what is unimportant to the success of his company, and so his responsiveness to anything that is out of line is far greater than that of the ordinary manager and considerably more acute than that of most chief executives.

This very sensitivity and perceptivity account for an apparent inconsistency in the way a Maverick Executive delegates responsibility. He often disregards the chain of command and dips his hand into details of problems that concern others far below him in the organization; subordinates then accuse him of meddling in their management. One board chairman made it clear to everyone on his staff that he had a "hunting license" to probe into every nook and cranny of his organization and to take whatever actions he deemed best, that he could do so without reference to company policy or any instructions the subordinate may have received from his immediate superiors. Similarly, a former president of General Motors, who was in the habit of checking on design details of the corporation's cars, once ordered a last-minute change in a design form that meant altering the entire production schedule. Theoretically these two top executives violated the mandates of good delegation, which discourages such interference by top executives. But in fact they were demonstrating the kind of management—one that involves constant surveillance—that a Maverick Executive habitually employs.

The Maverick never wholly entrusts anyone else in the organization with the make-or-break decisions. He believes, usually correctly, that only he has the total vision of the enterprise and that his lieutenants do not understand the relative importance of the elements of a situation. He knows that a flaw in a tiny detail can bring disaster in many ways—in costs, missed schedules, wrong staff appointments, misplaced managers, and in irretrievably wrong decisions. Because he cannot be everywhere at once, he inevitably misses most of the mistakes and must reconcile himself to live with them thereafter. But he never relaxes his vigilance in catching the little things that could result in big problems. He accepts the fact that the toughest decisions are his, and he knows that there is no such thing as relaxed leadership.

Many other interesting distinctions can be made between the Maverick Executive and the conventional entrepreneur or the hired professional manager. For example, as Copeman has pointed out,[4] companies managed by entrepreneurs have a significantly greater rate of growth than those managed by professional managers. This is probably owing not only to the entrepreneur's greater preoccupation with the daily workings of his enterprise, but also to the fact that he has greater freedom of action. His freedom, however, is based on his financial control of his company, whereas the Maverick Executive must achieve his goals by assuming authority through force of personality, drive, and manifest self-confidence. He does not ask for permission, he acts.

Unlike most professional managers, a Maverick

[4] George Copeman, *The Chief Executive and Business Growth* (New York: Leviathan House, 1971), pp. 338–339.

Executive, though he lacks financial control, is not afraid to take risks or affirmative action on his own. He wants freedom to act; he is far less accustomed to, or dependent upon, a highly structured, supportive environment. In fact, he is not comfortable in it. He does his best to avoid the limitations imposed by a large, regimented corporate organization where even the chief executive commonly finds his freedom restricted by the functions of an executive committee.

As a case in point, the chairman of General Motors must obtain approval if he wishes to spend more than $250,000 on a project, a relatively small sum for a company of such size. The executive committee's permission is required for projects costing up to $2.5 million, and beyond that figure the finance committee must be consulted. The chairman's role was stated by former Chairman Roche of General Motors: "My primary job is to reconcile different viewpoints and arrive at a consensus. Occasionally one must make individual decisions. In those cases, it is my responsibility."

A Maverick Executive finds it very difficult to operate within such restrictions of responsibility and authority. The exception, of course, would be the executive who has built the organization according to his own precepts and has installed his own controls. Unlike a conventional professional manager, a Maverick Executive does not accept restrictions on his decision-making authority if he can manage to avoid them. Like most entrepreneurs, he is more ego-involved in the business than is his professional counterpart. His objective is to manage the enterprise so that it succeeds and grows. And because he is not as cautious and conservative or as fearful as the professional manager, he is willing to take risks to accomplish his goals, even when it means overriding the executive committee of his board in order to continue a project. If he senses that a majority of the senior authorities oppose his recommendations, he may set these aside temporarily and advocate a different course. With this tactic, he hopes to persuade key members of the committee to back him up, especially if he is proposing some innovation that he is convinced will enable the company to succeed.

To a great extent, many of the qualities a Maverick Executive possesses *must* be contradictory. On the one hand, he must have basic self-confidence and, on the other, he must constantly anticipate trouble in his organization. Similarly, he must have great courage to be ruthless when necessary, often hurting and offending others, but he must also have enough magnetism and salesmanship to retain the confidence and loyalty of his subordinates. Above all, he must be the heroic father figure with whom his subordinates can establish a continuing, dependent, symbiotic relationship. This dependency is rarely overt, but in most instances it is very real. His subordinates trade their personal autonomy for the security and guidance he offers them.

Suppose, for example, our executive is confronted with the necessity to close down a plant that is the sole support of a community. He knows this will be economically painful to many people and may offend the social values of many of his subordinates and associates, thereby reducing his power over them. But if he is a Maverick Executive he has won the confidence of those who survive the closing—and retained his influence over them—by the way he has demonstrated to them that he, more than anyone else, will keep the company profitable and hence give them the personal security in their jobs that most of them so desperately, albeit not always consciously, need.

Because he has leadership by influence, the Maverick Executive is generally respected, trusted, admired, and emulated. He is the kind of leader most people—80 percent in my view—really want and need. He is an idealized father figure, an Old Testament Yahweh. As such, he must be seen as powerful and having high status and prestige in the company, the community, and the business world. He must not only offer his people security, but demand their obedience if he is to satisfy their submissive needs; he must provide them with approval and recognition when earned so as to gratify their ego needs; he must help the little man to provide for his need for support; he must be willing and able to bend the rules to satisfy the self-indulgence of his people.

This style of leadership, damned as autocratic management, is far from the participative, permissive, democratic management now so widely endorsed. But my observations indicate that people only *think* they want a democratic leadership that gives them full self-determination. Actually, they want only enough self-determination to save face. They want regimentation because it relieves them of responsibility, and they want forceful authority in their leadership in order to gratify their needs to be submissive. The autocratic leader also provides a scapegoat; if things go wrong, it is *his* fault. Because of their security needs, subordinates cannot generally tolerate ambiguity or weak leadership. It frightens them because it is not dependable and it provides no support. They *must* picture their leader (usually quite unrealistically) as the paragon they wish to believe he is—strong, decisive, tough, yet benign and benevolent.

Actually, a Maverick Executive is likely to fall a good deal short of any such ideal, for he is especially hindered by two weaknesses. One is a limited capacity for empathy, the other his limited capacity for introspection. Because he is insensitive to the feelings of others, he is generally unaware of people's needs, values, and expectations. Like most executives, he does not basically understand the powerful role these factors have in determining people's behavior. Intellectually, he knows the importance of recognizing the needs and expectations of his subordinates if he is to lead them effectively. He knows he should play different roles in dealing with different kinds of employees so as to satisfy their expectations and, at the same time, motivate them to yield their self-determination to him and accept his leadership. His major problem, however, is that he does not know exactly what these needs and expectations are. Even if he did, he could not quantify them, understand their individual significance, or exploit them to his advantage.

These are perhaps the most subtly difficult accomplishments for any chief executive. For the Maverick Executive they are even more difficult because of his limited capacity for introspection, a failing he shares with almost all other executives. Man's ability to see himself as he really is, to recognize, accept, and try to do something about his personal weaknesses is exceedingly rare. It may be the most demanding of all the tasks confronting any leader. It is a particularly hard one for the Maverick Executive because he is always in a hurry, he is not analytically inclined, and he is prone to wishful thinking. He finds it extremely difficult to be honest with himself. For example, he often fails to recognize that what he regards as his greatest asset may well be a glaring weakness. Most often, his delusion will be about his capacity either to delegate authority or to tolerate strong subordinates. He believes he delegates authority and gives lip service to the concept; in fact, he delegates little real authority and he cannot tolerate a strong subordinate.

Self-perception has frequently been postulated as an essential element in executive success. The manager–leader is told that he must make the most of his strengths and improve his weaknesses, that he must not indulge in self-deception. But for the Maverick Executive especially, the temptation to rationalize a course of action is almost irresistible. His self-deception is further compounded by the fact that the more intelligent and sophisticated he is, the more plausible and persuasive, albeit misleading, his defenses usually are. In reality, as any practicing psychiatrist can attest, few managers have much insight into their own motivations, and those who do have insight have many beliefs about themselves that are wildly inaccurate. To know oneself objectively is almost psychologically impossible. To act upon true insight is even more difficult.

An observer who cannot identify the characteristics of a Maverick Executive will not be able to recognize one when he meets him. Even the Maverick's close associates and subordinates, who do not see him as a whole, are quite likely to mistake his strengths for weaknesses and vice versa; their recognition that he is a mild hypomanic can be only superficial at best. Only by examining his track record and his characteristics objectively and in historical perspective can one be fairly sure of identifying him.

Some of the men of the past who exhibited a hyperkinetic makeup accomplished such outstanding feats in management that they became legends in the world of business leadership. One of the greatest was Theodore N. Vail, who helped Alexander Graham Bell set up the original telephone company. After a short time, Vail resigned in disgust when financiers usurped his management authority. He returned years later to become chairman of the American Telephone and Telegraph Company, establishing policies and procedures that set him far apart from his contemporaries. Among other things, Vail set the goal of service for the Bell System. And at a time when government control was considered anathema, he declared that the telephone company should be a government-regulated monopoly.

More recently, there was Robert Wood, chairman of Sears, Roebuck, whose perception of changes in marketing trends and customs, together with his courage in introducing retail stores, totally transformed

that company from primarily a mail-order house to a
retail-oriented enterprise. There was also the late
Alfred P. Sloan whose talents for organization and
development of managers transformed General Motors
from a collection of small companies in some disarray
into one of the greatest organized industrial complexes
in the world.

Today, mildly hypomanic, hyperkinetic Maverick
Executives are just as rare as they have always been,
but when their characteristics are known they are
visible enough, and there are a good many executives
who exhibit most if not all of the qualities required.
As a case in point, take the life and achievements of
Charles Kemmons Wilson, the chairman of Holiday
Inns, Inc., which by 1973 had over 1,400 motels in
50 states and 20 foreign countries or territories. A biographical sketch of Wilson in *Time* magazine described his behaviors and performance in terms that
indicated the wide variety of his qualities and capacities.[5] The characteristics of a Maverick Executive were
not attributed to Wilson by *Time*, but in my opinion
many of the statements in the article can be interpreted as evidence of such characteristics.

For example, the following statements from the
Time article could be seen as evidence of those qualities and capacities shown in parentheses after each
statement:

"A risk-taking entrepreneur in an age of prudent
professional managers, he is a visible refutation of the
common belief that a self-made man can no longer

[5] *Time* (July 12, 1972), pp. 77–82.

pile up great wealth in the modern, highly developed capitalist economy." (risk taking)

"The originator and chief executive of the chain is a bluff, zesty man who believes absolutely in the company motto that is imprinted on the necktie that he wears: 'It's a wonderful world.' " (great optimism)

"At work, Wilson runs mostly a one-man show, insisting on the last word in most major decisions and many small ones." (autocratic decision making)

"Says Wilson, 'I've been accused of lots of things, but never indecision!' " (decisiveness)

"Wilson generally sleeps about five hours a night and fortifies himself with catnaps the rest of the time." (hypomanic drive)

"For all his wealth, Wilson remains determinedly middle class in his values, tastes, and habits." (believer in the work ethic)

"When [his mother] lost her job during the Depression, Wilson, who had held part-time jobs almost since he could walk, quit high school and went to work for good." (self-taught by working experience)

"Holiday Inns has ridden out front by offering a host of new services that Wilson devised to lure more and more travelers." (innovation)

"He also has a sense of mission and sees the role of his company as more than a great money machine." (mission and perspective)

" 'When you get an idea,' he says, 'you've got to think of a reason for doing it, not of a reason for not doing it.' " (self-confidence and antianalytical approach)

"Wilson had a youth that was laced with adversity." (ability to overcome failures)

"Restlessly, Wilson dreamed of building a national franchise chain of 400 motels." (drive for a big goal)

"Wilson was among the first to foresee that the fast post-World War II rise in U.S. personal income would lead to a rapid expansion in both business and leisure travel." (foresight in business economics)

Although these statements suggest the basic nature and stature of a Maverick Executive, other important characteristics are not evident in this biographical sketch of Mr. Wilson. There is, for instance, no reference to some of those tougher aspects of the Maverick Executive which Mr. Wilson may or may not exhibit from time to time, such as a lack of empathy and the capacity for ruthlessness in certain situations. The lack of such characteristics may be critically significant for a Maverick Executive. Indeed the sobering fact is that an executive may possess a great many of the strengths of a Maverick Executive and yet be so deficient in one respect alone that his management eventually fails disastrously.

Paradoxically, perhaps the most serious weakness in a Maverick Executive, beyond his lack of insight into himself, stems from some of his definite strengths—his great drive and enthusiasm for meeting the immediate challenges and overcoming present obstacles. These preoccupations may prevent him from concentrating on how his organization is going to meet the changes and hazards and failures of the future. He is not likely to groom a strong executive as his successor, and in this respect he resembles the many famed figures of industry and politics who have failed to build organizations capable of enduring after they leave.

It is unrealistic, of course, to expect any human being to possess every one of the capacities for total success in management. But the Maverick Executive's extraordinary mixture of key characteristics undoubtedly qualifies him as a most promising candidate for such success.

HIS STYLE
OF MANAGEMENT

3

For the Maverick Executive, there is in effect only
one style of management: he is a benevolent autocrat.
Basically, he manages by centralizing power in his
hands, by carefully structuring the work of his subordinates, and by being a firm but fair disciplinarian.
It is a very effective style of management because it
provides the kind of leadership that most employees
want. Most subordinates recognize and accept him as
a man of integrity, as a self-confident leader who is
technically competent and a tough but fair taskmaster
as well. He engenders trust in his subordinates because
he provides them with the security they seek in their
work. They feel assured because he leaves little or no
doubt about what he wants them to do and how he
wants them to do it.

As a benevolent autocrat, the Maverick Executive
feels little need to delegate authority to his subordinates. Actually he delegates only to the few he considers qualified to make and carry out the kinds of
decisions he would make if he were in their shoes. But

he is also aware that even though these subordinates know what actions to take, he cannot always be sure that they will carry out his decisions unless he checks on them. He knows that close control of decision making is possible only when all positions and functions have been carefully structured so that employees know, first, what is expected of them and, second, that there will be a follow-up from above. In short, the Maverick Executive uses the style of management that now prevails in most corporate hierarchies.

He is a benevolent autocrat mainly by instinct. His nature, his attitudes, and his tremendous drive make him so. Although he is aware of other management styles, he knows little of their rationale; hence he tends to apply his own autocratic style indiscriminately, sometimes with quite negative results.

A great many executives have been led to believe that autocratic management, even mildly or benevolently autocratic, is wrong. They have been told that it is degrading for employees to submit to a system in which a hierarchy of supervisors hands down orders. Their negativism toward autocratic management has been nurtured by all the literature in recent years expounding other styles of management, particularly the participative-democratic style. But there is an almost universal error, in my opinion, in all the assumptions made about different styles or philosophies of management, and that is their almost total disregard for the wide diversity of human needs and preferences in situations where people are being supervised. Many behavioral scientists, for example, have fallen into this error by assuming three things about most people:

first, that they want the opportunity to "realize" themselves—that is, to set their own goals and work at their own pace; second, that employees resent restrictive job structuring and autocratic leadership; and third, that if employees are given a high degree of freedom and are encouraged to "do their thing" in their own way, they will be stimulated to improve their production and their morale will be improved.

These assumptions do not jibe with the sociological and psychological facts as I have observed them over many, many years. One fact, already noted, is that a substantial proportion of the population—75 percent or more—is inherently passive, dependent, submissive, and self-indulgent; in forthright terms, they do not like to work or submit to discipline. A great many people want and need structure in their jobs and seek support. A second major fact is that not many vocations and occupations provide the worker with much chance or freedom to determine for himself what to do and how to do it. Assembly-line operations and the military life are only extremes of this kind of rigidly structured work. A third fact is that there are many unpleasant jobs that simply have to be done and the people who have to do them have little opportunity to find their work satisfying or meaningful. The world being what it is, they work because they must eat.

No single style of management can be said to be applicable to all conditions and all types of subordinates; therefore, there is no right or wrong philosophy of leadership. The most appropriate management style is the one best suited to the nature of the work and to the kinds and values and expectations of the people employed in it. In addition to the benevolent-autocratic style of the Maverick Executive, there are four distinct types of supervision or philosophies of management that receive general recognition. A description of these styles should indicate why a Maverick Executive often has difficulties with certain groups of people who expect a different management style.

1. *The laissez-faire philosophy* is possible where a working group needs little structure or no supervision at all. Its members work within a very loose framework of directives and do whatever they think is necessary to accomplish the job. The leader of such a group has no line authority over the others; he is simply a *primus inter pares*, a first among equals. The group members are usually experienced and highly sophisticated, and have essentially similar backgrounds and interests. They engage in relatively unstructured activities—for example, original research and development work. Another example would be a group of professors or scholars under the dean of the university department—provided of course that the dean is not autocratic.

2. *The democratic-participative philosophy* is similar to the laissez-faire style, with members of the group largely setting their own goals, standards, and pace. But more structure and framework are provided here, and the leader is primarily a resource man or an adviser who sets the controls and objectives but does not usually establish the methods. His authority is minimal. Members of such a group are technically competent, experienced, and mature. An example

would be a group of engineers or scientists working with a fair degree of structure on a project where the objective has been established. Such employees are quite capable of disciplining themselves and can be given a great deal of freedom in their work. This is essentially Douglas McGregor's Theory Y in action.[1]

3. *The manipulative-inspirational, evangelical philosophy* is the "sell 'em on doing the job" approach. It has been very popular with sales organizations, especially where the staff is composed of "independent contractors" not subject to conventional discipline and on whom management has little direct leverage. For such groups a considerable amount of structure—usually somewhat confused and ambiguous—is provided, while the goals of the group (sales quotas, for instance) are imposed by top management and supervisors. There is little chance for employee participation. Managers try to get the employees to accept the goals and try to stimulate their performance through inspirational talks and various other efforts to "sell" compliance with the goals. For example, the "zero defects" programs in recent vogue are an effort to upgrade the quality of production by appealing to the employee's pride and sense of accomplishment.

4. *The autocratic-bureaucratic philosophy* imposes total, arbitrary (often mindless), and rigid structure on the activities of a group. Any participation by members of the group in any way is totally discouraged. The supervision is like the old-time military or

---

[1] Douglas McGregor, *The Human Side of Enterprise* (New York: McGraw-Hill Book Co., 1960).

maritime command, absolutely autocratic, arbitrary, and authoritarian, with unquestioning obedience demanded of the group. Even the questioning of any order is regarded as insubordination. This is McGregor's Theory X in action. Such supervision is appropriate for conscripts in the military or with employees who are very primitive in their reactions—say, a gang of laborers unloading a car of coal. Workers such as these are accustomed to autocratic supervision. Often they are incorrigibles who do not work voluntarily— members of chain gangs, for instance, who respond to nothing but an extremely autocratic type of control.

The benevolent-autocratic style of the Maverick Executive is a fifth style, applicable to activities that are partially or largely structured and where supervision is relatively close and authoritative. Here a certain amount of freedom is allowed. Employees are encouraged to make suggestions concerning their goals and working conditions, but final decisions on goals and standards are retained by the leader, who has full authority to discipline—even to terminate—members of the group. Usually this type of management is most appropriate where members of a group are involved in a wide variety of routine and well-structured activities—in a factory, office, or sales department, for example. These workers have relatively modest capacities so that they are apt to have well-defined needs for security and structure, and a predictable future in the company. Benevolent autocratic management provides the reassuring structure and support they need while giving them some opportunity to express their opinions and to participate to some extent in planning their work. It also offers some outlets for their grievances and, most important, the autocratic superior provides a scapegoat should anything go wrong.

The kind of management philosophy which will be applied depends on four factors: the personality of the chief executive, the structure and demands of the position, the character and values of the personnel, and the personality, values, standards, and expectations of the immediate supervisor. For example, if the position is relatively unstructured and if members of a group are mature, self-reliant, and emotionally well adjusted, they should respond well to democratic-participative or even laissez-faire supervision. If management has no real authority over the personnel, as in the case of independent contractors, such as specialty salesmen, it must use persuasive, manipulative, or inspirational supervision. If the employees are essentially passive, dependent, and need security, they require structure and support and are more comfortable and productive under a benevolent autocrat such as a Maverick Executive. And if they are primitive, or strongly aggressive, hostile, selfish, emotionally immature, or neurotic, they require very firm, even nakedly autocratic or military-type supervision.

The Maverick Executive, however, is not flexible enough to vary his management style to any great extent. He sticks to his benevolent-autocratic style because his knowledge of human behavior is superficial. He has an instinctive knowledge of how people conduct themselves within an organized structure, but his management philosophy is basically pragmatic. Having acquired competence in management at many levels, he is convinced of the constant need for applying discipline to people in an organization. Since he has little understanding of what makes people behave as they do and little acquaintance with human psychopathology, he ignores the fact that about 75 percent of the population are anxious and fearful and 60 percent have other emotional problems which are the roots of conflict that produce many of the serious people problems he has to face.

Yet the Maverick Executive does know that the currently prevailing organizational system in business is hierarchical, that responsibility is centralized in a relatively small number of executives and supervisors. He knows, too, that as many as 90 percent of the positions in any company are almost totally regimented and structured and have minimal risk-taking or decision-making responsibilities. In his experience, he has found that the most successful business organizations have centralized control of final decision making in corporate headquarters, so that a small group of managers—from five to ten—can administer even a billion-dollar enterprise. He has also learned that if a major decision is pushed down the hierarchy ladder, it is almost always sent back up to the top level for final decision. The Maverick Executive is aware that although the control from the top cannot be blindly autocratic, as it is in military organizations, still the top executives must be strongly autocratically oriented if anything is to be accomplished.

If the Maverick Executive were truly perceptive about employees, he would recognize that there are five distinct classes of personnel in an organization, each of which has its own needs, aspirations, and problems; and that the style of management that is suitable with one of these classes may have little or no effect on other classes of personnel. In descending order, the five classes may be described as follows:

1. *The entrepreneur manager* (or, very rarely, two equally strong managers) at the apex of the corporate pyramid. Here is where the company's objectives, long-range plans, and comprehensive organization structures are determined, where all major decisions are made. It is the source of initiative for growth and administration.

2. *The upper level executives.* These are the top-line administrators, the vice presidents and general managers who make the operating (but not policy) decisions and carry on the day-to-day functions of production, sales and marketing, finance, accounting and record keeping, research and development, and special services such as public relations, personnel, industrial relations, legal work, and so on.

3. *The line managers in middle and lower levels* of management. These are the supervisors and department heads of the corporation's various functions and activities. They make the necessary operating decisions in their areas, supervise the work of others, and serve as communications centers—and also as communications barriers.

4. *The staff employees* who perform specialized functions. They are the technicians who make some technical decisions in their own areas but who have no supervisory responsibilities outside their depart-

ments. Their primary function is to advise and recommend or to maintain records.

5. *The monthly-, weekly-, and hourly-rated employees* who are at the base of the corporate pyramid. This group is composed of all other employees under supervision; their decisions are strictly structured and generally trivial.

Ordinarily, the differences in these five kinds of personnel are stated in terms of income, status and authority, education, clothes, speech, and other cultural factors. But there are far more critical differences to be noted, such as those individual differences among people as to what they specifically want in their jobs. Some want freedom to make their own decisions, some do not. There are also great differences in the demands of various positions. Some offer a high degree of freedom, independence, and autonomy while others—and there are many more of these—are highly regimented, lacking in challenge, and even degrading.

These are not the aspects, however, that concern the Maverick Executive. He concentrates on the fundamental differences in the *structuring* of positions. Many chief executives fail to recognize the extent of the employees' need for structure with its concomitant guidance, support, and freedom from responsibility. "Structure" here means that a position is so defined and supervised that the incumbent knows exactly what he may or may not do and hence has practically no risk-taking decisions to make. Only a few positions—those at or near the apex of the management pyramid—are relatively unstructured. Nearly all lesser jobs in business and industry are highly structured and have guidelines to cover nearly every contingency.

For the Maverick Executive, structuring is imperative for five reasons: First, it insures uniformity of action, which, in a large, widely dispersed organization, is imperative. Second, it makes supervision easier for both subordinate and supervisor because instructions are usually quite precise. Nothing is more anxiety provoking to the typical worker than ambiguity and uncertainty. Third, structuring relieves the incumbent of responsibility; all that is required of him is that he faithfully follow the instructions that are given him directly or are to be found in the "book." Fourth, a well-structured activity demands little initiative and minimal creativity (although occasionally some is possible *within* the established guidelines), and fifth, it demands practically no decision making. This last feature is the one that makes regimented positions not only bearable but even strongly appealing to many people. Most people who work for salaries and wages do not wish to take responsibility if in so doing they might jeopardize their job security or lay themselves open to criticism. They need a superior to blame when things go wrong. This correlates clearly with the fact that most activities below the division or department-head level are from 90 to 100 percent structured, requiring practically no imaginative or risk-taking decisions whatever. The fact that structuring exists in every type of enterprise—business, religious, military, and governmental—suggests that it satisfies a very deeply entrenched human need.

The Maverick Executive, when he becomes the

Chief Executive Officer, occupies probably the least structured position in any organization. He sets the policies, takes the risks, and provides the drive and initiative for the entire organization. His position is structured only to the degree that industry practices, government and company policies, bankers, and his directors may limit and control his activities. However, he has the ultimate responsibility, because his desk is where the buck stops.

The upper-level administrators and executives who report directly to the Maverick Executive work in semistructured positions. They carry out his directives within the framework of policy he has established, thus relieving him of detail. They submit ideas to him for consideration, and they serve as a sounding board for his ideas.

Those in the lower echelons—the line, staff, and monthly- and hourly-rated employees—are in almost totally structured positions. The Maverick Executive does not expect them to make any significant decisions on their own; they are not expected to initiate things, but are expected to follow the directives of their bosses as faithfully as possible. They are the "hewers of wood and the carriers of water" through whom the work of the organization gets done along daily routines established for them. The positions they hold require little more than technical skills and the usual middle-class virtues, such as industry and loyalty and the willingness and ability to work steadily within a framework of policies and procedures.

The benevolent autocracy of a Maverick Executive

should be distinguished from the kind of autocracy commonly found in bureaucrats. It is simply the difference between a strong autocrat and a weak autocrat. A strong autocrat, like the Maverick Executive, is very aggressive, hard-driving, inner-directed, and self-reliant. Although he is not a tyrant, he is so preoccupied with his other interests and problems that he does not give much thought to his employees and, indeed, has little feeling for them. He is autocratic in his relations with others simply because he has learned from experience that this is the best way for him to get things done.

The weak bureaucratic autocrat, on the other hand, is the typical overstriver. He may be intelligent, loyal, conscientious, and technically well qualified, but behind his authoritative front he has an overwhelming need for security. He is psychologically weak. At heart he is a dependent, fearful, anxious person who compensates for his insecurities by assuming an arbitrary authoritarian exterior, often with great emphasis on his status and symbols. Yet he adheres compulsively to prevailing practices, procedures, and policies. He must always have rules to go by, because rules or instructions from a superior relieve him of responsibility. Given these supports, he is a tower of strength.

It should be noted here that the adverse reaction to autocratic management is not caused by autocracy itself. Employees resent *weak* autocracy because that kind of management creates anxiety in them. It creates anxiety because the executive is recognized as unpredictable and unreliable, a boss who will look for scapegoats. All these symptoms are born of his underlying weaknesses. He is the typical "bull of the woods."

One of the most distinctive ways in which a strong autocrat differs from a weak one is how he issues orders. The weak autocrat simply issues orders and demands absolute obedience; the strong one, like the Maverick Executive, because he leads by influence, usually "suggests" the action to be taken. And though he does not ask his subordinates what they think should be done, he may encourage their participation in planning a course of action. Furthermore, he skillfully encourages his subordinates to participate *prior* to the decision-making process, although he knows the ultimate decision will be his.

It is interesting to note that the need for autocracy in management was clearly recognized even by Douglas McGregor, perhaps the most ardent champion of participative management. In 1954, when he resigned after serving six years as president of Antioch College (and six years before the publication of his major work, *The Human Side of Enterprise*), McGregor confessed how wrong he had been in his pre-Antioch assumptions about the role an executive has to play. In an essay "On Leadership" he wrote:

> It took the direct experience of becoming a line executive, and meeting personally the problems involved, to teach me what no amount of observation of other people could have taught. I believed, for example, that a leader could operate successfully as a kind of adviser to his organization. I thought

I could avoid being a "boss." Unconsciously, I suspect, I hoped to duck the unpleasant necessity of making difficult decisions, of taking responsibility for one course of action among many uncertain alternatives, of making mistakes and taking the consequences. I thought that maybe I could operate so that everyone would like me—that "good human relations" would eliminate all discord and disagreement.

I could not have been more wrong. It took a couple of years, but I finally began to realize that a leader cannot avoid the exercise of authority any more than he can avoid responsibility for what happens to his organization. . . . A colleague recently summed up what my experience has taught me in these words: "A good leader must be tough enough to win a fight, but not tough enough to kick a man when he is down." This notion is not in the least inconsistent with humane, democratic leadership. Good human relations develop out of strength, not out of weakness.[2]

In those last two sentences McGregor apparently tried to soften the implications of his own experience. But then he added this revealing sentence: "I am still trying to understand and practice what is implied in my colleague's statement."

The virtues of a benevolent-autocratic management for most activities are well known and practiced by

[2] Douglas McGregor, *Leadership and Motivation* (Cambridge, Mass.: M.I.T. Press, 1966), pp. 66–70.

all Maverick Executives, for they have learned the disillusioning truth that the real interests of most employees lie outside their jobs. They do not really want to work or try to improve themselves if it requires effort, and they do not want responsibility. Most simply, they want a safe, secure, regimented job and someone to tell them what to do. They know, too, that the use of pronouncements, warnings, and threats —the usual tactics of the overstriving bureaucrat or autocrat—is simply ineffective in influencing the attitudes and behavior of most employees. It simply stimulates them to exercise their "strategies of independence," such as passive resistance.

Behavioral scientists to the contrary notwithstanding, workers' apathy and antagonism toward their jobs does not come from the nature of work in plants and offices. One recent study states that about 90 percent of workers say their work is satisfying to them and they like it.[3] In another study, many plant employees were found to be satisfied with work that intellectuals regard as boring because *"workers are not a cross section of the population, but are a select group.* There is a greater selection of jobs by workers than is supposed."[4] A worker in effect screens each new job; he tries it out for several days or weeks to see if it suits him before deciding whether or not to stay. Manage-

[3] Thomas C. Sorensen, "Do Americans Like Their Jobs?" *Parade Magazine,* June 3, 1973.

[4] Mitchell Fein, PE, *Rational Approaches to Productivity,* Pub. #5, Monograph Series "Work Measurement and Methods" (Engineering Div., American Institute of Industrial Engineers, Inc., 1974), p. 2.

ment, of course, also decides whether the worker will be kept beyond the trial period. These two screening processes cull out the potentially dissatisfied worker.

The Maverick Executive's style of management is not acceptable to all employees, of course. Although most of them like to be told what to do, some do not, and since people do tend to gravitate toward the style of management that is most compatible to them, a change of management style can be terribly traumatic to employees. Those who object to structure and authority are bound to be resentful if their permissive-participative supervisor is replaced by an autocrat; on the other hand, permissive-participative management is certain to produce anxiety in employees who are accustomed to, are dependent upon, and are satisfied with autocratic supervision. However, since people who are compatible with benevolent autocracy can be found at all levels of a corporation, up to and including top management, this particular style continues to be the most generally useful and widely employed in industry. And despite the fact that many intellectuals, behavioral scientists, and young people are expressing strong resentment against hierarchical authority, the Maverick Executive's management style promises to continue being as effective as it has always been in producing successful corporate performance as well as satisfied subordinates.

·

HOW HE LIKES
HIS MANAGEMENT TEAM

4

It has become a popular shibboleth of management theory that the really informed and competent executive invariably builds a management team to assist him. The Maverick Executive knows better. The idea that a management team, per se, is an absolute essential in the operation of a successful enterprise is silly in his opinion, even though he is aware that the idea has become so well accepted that few now question it. He knows there are no clear and unambiguous definitions of what constitutes a managing team, which he has heard wishfully described as a unit that is synergistic and well unified, composed of technically qualified personnel who are also aggressive "tigers," each of whom may be seen as a potential chief executive.

In practice, as the Maverick Executive knows, many management teams are not very well qualified technically and are rarely well integrated and synergistic. Few can boast of "tigers" and even fewer are composed of potential chief executives. The Maverick

Executive knows that the "management team" is usually another designation for the executive committee, senior executives who obediently carry out the chief's directives in the day-to-day running of the business, submit a few ideas to him, and serve mainly as his sounding board. The Maverick Executive is very skeptical of teams because, although he's read about them, he has seen few that accomplished much constructively to his way of thinking. To him, in fact, an ideally balanced management team is a fiction; in his highly realistic view, no such team exists.

Moreover, a Maverick Executive is well aware that if a management team were actually composed mainly of dynamic and aggressive "tigers," the group could be dangerously disruptive. He knows they would be a serious source of trouble, not only because there would be rivalry among them but because such aggressive managers would compete so strenuously for his job as chief executive that they might well undermine him. At the very least, he would have to spend a disproportionate amount of time constraining their uncooperative tendencies and the chaos that would be caused by each one's compulsively seeking his own separate goal. The centrifugal forces thus generated could totally destroy the enterprise. For this reason few management teams include more than one or at most two really strong men.

In one organization, a clique of old timers ganged up on the president, a relative newcomer, and attempted to frustrate his every innovation. Their principal weapon was passive resistance. The technique they used was to greet every new project with great enthusiasm and then allow it to wither on the vine. Their chief objective was to get the president out— either by frustrating him to the point where he would leave voluntarily or by so impairing his performance that the owners would terminate him. Realizing that it was a matter of personal survival, the president took the only course open to him: he terminated four of the five members of his executive committee at once. The action was a severe one, but it was the only way he could insure his own survival in the company.

To the Maverick Executive, the working management team consists simply of a group of managers, most of whom are not aggressive enough to be disruptive, who can really collaborate and cooperate with him in accomplishing what *he* wishes to be done. He recognizes that such a group, while not composed of "barn burners," can make invaluable, positive contributions to his success. In fact, without them, he cannot succeed in applying the technique of management by exception. He knows there must be two kinds of managers in such a group: some who are line managers in administrative, decision-making jobs, and others who are staff managers whose job is to advise, recommend, and keep records.

The differences between the two kinds are marked. The line executives hold jobs that require getting things done, often with responsibilities for profit and loss; they *decide and act* and are responsible for basic operating activities. There are only two truly line activities: production and sales. Staff executives, on the other hand, include either contemplative types— the thinkers and planners who are usually technicians in industry today—or people who are essentially clerks concerned with record keeping and information storage and retrieval. Often they are technicians or specialists in a narrow field, such as accounting, law, finance, or research and development. They recommend to and advise their superiors but give orders (in a line sense) only to those under them in their departments. A separate category of functional or staff manager may be found where a technical specialist is supervised by some higher-up at headquarters but reports directly to his local manager. This occurs chiefly in accounting departments where division controllers conform to rules established and supervised by the corporate controller but report in a line capacity to the division manager.

Ideally both line and staff executives perform better if they are somewhat like their opposites. But the Maverick Executive knows that he is better off with a minimum number of line managers, especially at high levels in the company, because this kind is most likely to conspire against him in an attempt to undermine his authority. While staff managers can also be dangerous to him, they are more easily constrained by a Maverick Executive since they frequently lack the line manager's courage.

The Maverick Executive tends to be always slightly paranoid regarding his line managers and tries to limit and control their authority. He watches their activities closely and is always careful to make it difficult for them to establish themselves in positions where they can exercise power over him. In one company, for example, the chief engineer blackmailed his management for years by threatening to go to a competitor and take his staff with him.

The Maverick Executive, like most people, needs someone with whom he can talk out his problems and his plans. His selection of a confidant is usually fortuitous, someone with whom he simply happens to be congenial and compatible and who has skills the Maverick Executive feels he can use. He may be a member of the executive committee, a fellow director, the company's attorney, an old retainer, or even an outsider, perhaps a consultant. If he happens to be an employee, he often serves as a confidential source of intelligence and as an informal channel of upward, downward, and outward communication. Whatever else he happens to be, the confidant becomes an integral member of the Maverick's entourage.

The very informal relationship with the confidant may or may not be stable and enduring, depending upon the Maverick Executive's personality, especially the extent of his paranoid tendencies. Since the confidant is chosen on a purely emotional, nonrational basis, he may prove to be either an invaluable asset or a costly liability. This is because his proximity to the throne often gives him tremendous influence and leverage in matters of policy and administration. If so inclined, he can easily become an *éminence grise* in management who can either appreciably improve or seriously depress company morale. He may make positive contributions to a Maverick Executive's thinking or simply be a sounding board or an outlet through which his chief achieves emotional catharsis.

In selecting his close advisers, the Maverick Executive is astutely concerned with building his "office." He recognizes that, in addition to his line administrators, three types of staff managers should make up his "office" to constitute a broad working staff. The first group includes his personal staff—that is, his secretary (or secretaries) who will have little official status and will handle minor details for him.

The second group includes his "assistants to," or aides-de-camp, the members of his general staff. Although organizational planners often disapprove of such personnel, who have no real authority in the company, a Maverick Executive finds them extremely useful. They draft memoranda for his signature, issue his instructions, provide communications up and down the line, supervise his confidential records, and assist his line subordinates. In short, their main function is to help their chief in integrating and coordinating the activities of the company on many levels.

The third group includes his staff specialists—for example, the heads of such ancillary service functions as finance, treasury (bank relations), accounting, taxes, law, personnel, research and development, public relations, and so on. These people may act as advisers to the chief in major policy matters, in government relations, for instance. While specialists have authority for running their own departments, they may issue no direct instructions to any line personnel at any level. However, they are often responsible for monitoring the activities of personnel who report directly to line managers, thus helping to insure compliance with company policies and regulations. They also perform a variety of specialized staff functions such as the accumulation and analysis of data and the supervision of training activities.

Obviously the task of developing a really effective management team is not simply a matter of picking a few key line executives and technical specialists and letting them build staffs on their own. The Maverick Executive realizes that staffing is one of his most difficult and critically important tasks. Unfortunately, like 95 percent of all executives, he is not aware that every job has five critical dimensions, or parameters, and that each job is, to some extent, unique, differing from every other job in five major respects: First, each job has its own requirements and involves certain special factors: working conditions (such as working hours, amount of travel, possible necessity for relocation), various kinds of co-workers, customers to be dealt with, markets to be run. Second, each job differs in the degree of its structure—the magnitude of the decisions to be taken and the closeness of the supervision provided. Third, each job differs in the degree of probable compatibility between the values, expectations, temperament, and competence of those who supervise it and of those who perform it. Fourth, each job has a different earnings potential. And fifth, each job differs in its opportunities for advancement. (Is it a "career" or dead-end job, or one that represents another step on the ladder of advancement?) Because of his ignorance of these factors, the Maverick Executive makes serious errors in the selection and placement of key personnel.

Since every human being is unique in his own way, beginning with his fingerprints, the essence of effective staffing lies in matching the many parameters of the job with the different characteristics of the incumbent. This matching process is necessary whether the employee is being upgraded from within the organization or brought in from the outside. There are no shortcuts in this difficult job of staffing, if it is to be done properly. It is costly, time consuming, and frustrating and requires all the expertise it can get. No executive can do this personally, so he usually assigns the job to his personnel staff or hires some outside specialist to do it.

Too often, however, a Maverick Executive like many other executives will undertake his own search for someone to serve on his staff, and in doing so he usually makes the most common selection error of all: He simply picks someone who either appeals to him or has been successful at a lower level or has attained unusual visibility. For, supremely confident himself, he does not know that success at one level does not necessarily qualify an executive for advancement to a higher level, or that skill at self-promotion does not guarantee skill as a manager. Each type and level of position requires its own special constellation of skills, traits, attributes, motivations, values, and personality makeup, especially self-confidence.

The Maverick Executive's insensitivity to people also blinds him to the importance of providing competent supervision for every position. Proper supervision is as important as all the subordinates' qualifications put together. In fact, the competence, personality, standards, values, and expectations of the supervisor can totally offset the performance of even able candidates. Yet the Maverick Executive is not only unaware of the damage that incompetent supervisors can do to competent subordinates; he is also ignorant of this basic, unfortunate fact about personnel management: Nearly always, the person least qualified to assess a candidate's potential for advancement is his own immediate boss.

Theoretically no one should be a better judge of a subordinate's competence than his immediate supervisor. After all, the supervisor works with him every day and has an opportunity to observe his strengths and weaknesses at close hand. Unfortunately, it does not work out in practice, because there are almost always at least some areas of incompatibility or overcompatibility—whether in temperament or values—between a supervisor and each subordinate which can nullify objectivity for both of them.

Thus a Maverick Executive is usually a poor judge of his subordinates' competence to assess the promotability of the people under their supervision. Such assessments are notoriously unreliable. For example, a railway executive I know was greatly taken with one of his officers and described him as "perfect, the best we've ever had, and I'd like to have a hundred more like him." When asked why he thought the officer was so good, the executive replied, "He never takes any action without asking me first."

A final aspect of staffing which the Maverick Executive now must take into account is conformity with the law relating to minorities, women, and those between the ages of 40 and 65. His strong personal biases and prejudices about managerial competence will have to be tailored to comply with the standards set by the U.S. Supreme Court in March 1971. The Court then held by a vote of 8 to 0 (in *Griggs* v. *Duke Power Co.*) that an employer cannot discriminate against members of a minority group (women, blacks, the middle-aged) by refusing to hire or promote them because they fail to meet his hiring and promotion standards unless those standards are related to performance on the job. This ruling affirmed the guidelines on selection procedures as interpreted by the Equal Opportunity Employment Commission under the Civil Rights Act of 1964. The extent of these complications has been presented in a recent study by The Conference Board.[1]

A Maverick Executive, for example, would certainly not approve of one of the conclusions reached by staffing experts at AT&T, as reported in The Conference Board study. That giant corporation has found that "it now makes sense to experiment with developing fast-track vertical staffing processes for rank-and-file employees that will link on to its fast-track managerial program so that any especially able employee who wants to do so can continue to move rapidly through new learning experiences at higher organization levels without encountering an age differential problem." In short, every able employee—not just young, college-educated trainees—should be promoted up the management ladder. Although a Maverick Executive is usually not a college man, and although he

---

[1] Ruth G. Schaeffer, *Staffing Systems: Managerial and Professional Jobs* (New York: The Conference Board, 1972).

himself rises on his own fast track, he does not promote young managers who can challenge his authority. Also, he is aware that the advancement potential of most employees is limited to three echelons.

As businesses grow they, like organisms, pass through developmental stages, and the Maverick Executive may have serious trouble adapting his staffing to the stage at which he finds his enterprise at the time he takes over. At least five stages can be delineated: The beginning entrepreneurial stage (less than 100 people); the transitional stage (100–200 people); the mature stage (500–10,000 people); the bureaucratic stage (over 10,000 people); and the moribund stage (which occurs in all sizes of companies).

The Maverick Executive, insensitive to people, often does not recognize that the character of the staffing needs undergoes an almost total change as a company passes from youth and vigor to maturity to rigidity and finally to almost total ossification. The type of person who feels happy and challenged in a young, relatively unstructured, growing business would be ill at ease in a mature organization and unhappy in a bureaucratic one. Conversely, a frightened, anxious individual is uncomfortable in a young, unstructured enterprise, but happy and secure in a bureaucratic or moribund one. There will be a 180-degree shift from practically no structure at all in a young, growing organization to a rigid, all-encompassing structure in a company that is on its way to extinction. Such a shift must be accompanied by a corresponding shift in the quality of staff, going from personnel who need little structure in their work and resent its imposition to personnel who do need structure and welcome it as something that increases their sense of security.

Since a Maverick Executive overlooks these creeping changes in the character of his staff, or its status when he takes over, he usually finds himself in trouble. He may, for example, become extremely active in a new enterprise and expect all those working with him to be dynamic generalists, expert in several fields and needing little guidance and support. He is then dismayed to find that as the organization grows, he can no longer depend on the men around him except within the limited scope of their specialties. He has lost his daring innovators. But he still expects them to be as competent in the broad areas as the people he had before, and his appraisal of these subordinates is therefore distorted, without his knowing why.

The most obvious case is that of a powerful chief executive and founder of a company who continues, in spite of the growth of his enterprise and the change in his managers, to demand the kind of versatility in his subordinates that he was used to when the company was very small. As a result, he may continue to fire his more dependent executives and replace them with others in the vain hope that these new men will give him the adaptability he is looking for.

One Maverick Executive I knew was a generalist in every sense. He had been trained as an engineer, but he had broad experience in production, accounting, finance, and sales. All these aspects of management were simple and easy for him to understand, and he was very intolerant of specialists and technicians whose expertise was limited to one or two narrow fields. Versatility was his watchword. When it became apparent that a key member of his staff "didn't have it," out he went. As a result, the turnover in his management staff was excessive and as the word got around in the business community that the president was hard to please, it became increasingly difficult to recruit qualified replacements.

The Maverick Executive also tends to be unaware that his management staff needs are certain to change in character, through internal rivalries and conflicts within his management team as well as external influences—political, technological, and economic. (At the same time, such influences usually affect his own main function as chief executive very little, whether he manages a $50,000 company or a $5 billion business.) The extent of such influences as a whole must necessarily be unequal, but they will inevitably have a disruptive effect on the nature of the team he is supervising; and the goals, competence, and personalities of the key individuals he is working with will tend to change, thereby changing the nature of his team.

One result of such changes is that the Maverick Executive may be forced to introduce additional staff services in order to maintain his effectiveness as a chief executive. He may have to add managers to increase his controls or the coordination of his directives or the communication within the company. As a rule, when companies grow larger, their weakest areas—staff functions of record keeping, planning and control, coordination, communications, and the special functions of law, research, personnel, and public relations—are given the greatest reinforcement and are extended disproportionately. Because performance is much more difficult to appraise in staff activities than it is in line operations, the number of staff employees tends to increase geometrically as companies grow, while line personnel increase arithmetically.

For a Maverick Executive this means that while he is pushing the firm to grow and grow, staff proliferation readily becomes excessive, and this growth gives rise to such great numbers of bureaucratic "emperors" that Parkinson's famous law becomes operable. Therefore the prospects for developing and maintaining an efficient management team may not seem particularly bright under a Maverick Executive.

However, while he may not avoid the staff problems he must inevitably face as his organization grows, the Maverick Executive has his typical ways to offset these unfavorable developments. His solution is simple and often rather painful: He ruthlessly cuts back on any staff or line functions that he finds unnecessary or overblown, and he makes it his business from time to time to discover just when such conditions exist. This kind of pruning is extremely distasteful to most executives, but a Maverick Executive accepts it as an essential responsibility in the interest of maintaining his company's health.

HIS TWO MAJOR
BLIND SPOTS

5

One of the most memorable features about the Maverick Executive is that he is able to succeed phenomenally as a chief executive even though he constantly exhibits extreme weaknesses in some of the most important functions of management. His lack of empathy, his overoptimism, his impatience, and his other failings cause him to blunder repeatedly in his dealings with people. His incompetence shows up very markedly in two areas: the evaluation of personnel and the establishment of communication channels. Though he is usually unaware of it, in each of these tasks the Maverick Executive needs a great deal of help and there are definite ways and means by which his organization may be protected from his shortcomings.

Consider first the ways a Maverick Executive evaluates his immediate subordinates. Like most chief executives, he believes that an employee's career is determined primarily by the textbook work ethic and by the Horatio Alger virtues of diligence, competence, dedication, submissiveness to authority, and willingness to make sacrifices. More often than not, he hires or promotes a manager on the basis of one or a combination of the following grounds: technical expertise (which is relatively easy to measure), length of service, loyalty to the company (sometimes a synonym for docility), recommendation by a peer or by a "search" agency (whose main interest is in placing the candidate), superficial contacts ("I met him at a party"), personal charisma and skill at self-selling, nepotism, sheer desperation (he is the only one available, the only one anybody could think of or "the best of the worst"), word-of-mouth reputation, or off-the-cuff recommendations from business associates.

In using these criteria the Maverick Executive demonstrates how far he is from understanding the techniques and pitfalls of appraising an employee's competence. And he is even more ignorant of what the true determinants of an employee's progress are. He does not recognize that an employee's career is primarily determined not by his qualities or performance but by his supervisor's perception of the nature of the employee's accomplishments and the supervisor's *estimate* of the impact of those accomplishments on the supervisor's *own* personal status and security. Exceptional competence on an employee's part, for instance, may be a fatal handicap if his supervisor is especially anxious or fearful. Under a lazy supervisor, the employee may not be downgraded and dismissed, but he is not likely to be promoted either; his boss usually needs his services too badly.

Moreover, a Maverick Executive will be unaware

that these inequities in appraisal are rarely willful or malicious. Most assessments are made in good faith; almost always, the person who does the appraising has sincere, comfortable rationalizations for his findings. His conscience never bothers him; he has convincing, often perfectly logical reasons for what he does, and if he is charged with bias, he becomes indignant. The injustice of this is that the boss acts as prosecutor, judge, and jury rolled into one, and usually he is doing so outside the knowledge of *his* bosses. There is also the critical—and sometimes unbelievably cruel—fact that in cases of dispute about an appraisal, those in management (and the Maverick Executive is no exception) invariably back the supervisor, no matter how biased or how viciously pejorative his judgments may be.

Because the Maverick Executive knows so little about people, he is blind to the many ways his subordinates will distort their appraisals on the basis of personal compatibility. The degree of personal compatibility between the supervisor and a subordinate inevitably colors the appraisal of performance; if the two are compatible, the assessment will be favorable; if they are incompatible, or if the subordinate is perceived as a threat, the evaluation will be negative. Since practically all assessments of this kind are subjective judgments, they tend to be spurious. Some judgments exclude negative points about a compatible subordinate who may be manifestly incompetent; the supervisor's desire to say something favorable is so strong that he unintentionally omits critical elements. He may say, "Joe is our best design engineer and has been with us for twenty-five years." But he then fails to qualify this statement by saying that Joe is the best design engineer when he is sober.

If the Maverick Executive were perceptive about people he would realize how completely the factor of compatibility determines the judgments of supervisors as to the kind of employees they recommend for raises and promotions. More often than not, compatibility is the key to any employee's advancement and, to insure it, he must meet three criteria:

—He must be technically competent to the extent that his performance conforms to his supervisor's expectations. This is not as easy as it sounds, since there are vast differences in standards.

—His values must be reasonably consonant with those of his supervisor, which usually means the values of the work ethic.

—He must not be so well qualified that he threatens the supervisor's own sense of job security.

In addition to these obstacles to objective appraisals, there are a great many other sources of error to be found in the assessments of subordinates by their superiors. The Maverick Executive does not recognize these errors by his subordinates simply because he consciously or unconsciously commits all of them himself at one time or another. Here are the most common:

1. Executives are willing to rate subordinates who may be virtually unknown to them, even after years of daily association.

2. Executives are often unwilling to take the time or make the effort to analyze their subordinates thoroughly.

3. The temperaments of raters color their assessments so differently, from overfriendly to overcritical, that the results are largely a matter of chance.

4. Ratings often show a "halo" effect. If a subordinate is liked and is compatible, he is seen to excel in nearly every trait; if he is disliked or is incompatible, he is seen to be deficient in nearly every trait.

5. Raters are overly influenced by the latest happenings in employee performance. They tend to give too much weight, for example, to the fact that a subordinate has just had a great success or failure.

6. Ratings frequently exhibit the "sunflower" effect in that raters give their bosses information that will not be embarrassing to themselves as supervisors. They conceal incompetence with this kind of remark: "None of my men is less than 100 percent or I wouldn't keep him."

7. Raters tend to second-guess their bosses by telling them what they think they want to hear; for example, a rater will tell the president how competent his son is, without regard for actual performance.

8. Raters often play politics; they may, for example, use high or favorable ratings to curry the favor of their subordinates.

9. Raters are reluctant to make adverse ratings because they fear personal confrontation and discussion with the subordinate, or, even if a personal discussion is unnecessary, fear they will be identified as the one who made the unfavorable rating.

10. Ratings may be used for ulterior purposes. A rater may, for example, give a better or worse rating than is deserved in order to justify giving or withholding raises or promotions for unrelated reasons.

11. Performance standards vary from rater to rater. Frequently the very words used to describe performance mean totally different things to different raters.

12. A rater may have strong personal prejudices. He may sincerely believe, for example, that "all Swedes are squareheads."

13. A rater's sense of propriety may inhibit him from making a critical or adverse judgment because to do so would not be "nice" and would conflict with his desire to help a subordinate.

14. Some raters lack analytical ability and fail to see causal relationships. Many are inclined to make excuses for their people.

15. Raters tend to be indecisive. In their reluctance to rate either high or low, they exhibit a "central tendency," preferring to stick to averages. This provides them with a built-in escape hatch; if the subject subsequently succeeds or fails, they cannot be faulted, since they have not said he was either good or bad.

16. Raters are prone to wishful thinking—for example, "Everyone is promotable, perhaps in five years."

17. Colleagues tend to be mutually protective and are reluctant to say anything adverse about each other. The reasoning is, if I don't reveal *his* weaknesses, he'll do the same for me.

In addition to all these causes of unreliable ratings there are other barriers to objective assessments. Very few positions above the production, clerical, or sales levels are of such a nature that genuinely objective quantitative measures or criteria of performance can be obtained. This is particularly true of staff positions and most middle management positions. How, for example, is the work of a public relations director assessed? By the number of times the company president's picture appears in the paper?

It is no wonder, then, that even chief executives who, unlike the Maverick Executive, are interested in their subordinates, know so little about the really vital aspects of appraisal. However, there is one fact that considerably reduces the size of the problem of finding and promoting good managers. This is the fact that the distribution of competence in employees at each level in an enterprise follows a normal, bell-shaped curve—that is, regardless of whether the employees are executives or factory workers, only 10 to 20 percent can be expected to be exceptionally well qualified, imaginative, productive, skilled in their specialty, natural leaders. So the Maverick Executive has to identify only the ones who are in that top 10 to 20 percent and then have their specific strengths and weaknesses assessed.

Because of their built-in errors and distortions, conventional rating-based appraisal programs will be of no help in finding the most promising subordinates. However, there are two distinct evaluation techniques that notably improve the Maverick Executive's chances of penetrating the personality masks of his subordinates and finding out their true nature.

One of these techniques is the systematic testing and interviewing of potential executives in an assessment center. Developed by AT&T, this system has been adopted by more than a dozen other large corporations including IBM, General Electric, and Sears, Roebuck as well as some government agencies. Assessment centers are based in part on the stress-situation techniques of the Office of Strategic Services developed during World War II. In this program candidates are subjected to tests, interviews, and various simulated business games, job situations, and problems such as the in-basket procedure. During leaderless group discussions or dialogues, candidates are watched by a panel of their bosses and trained observers.

Most assessment centers cover all the areas that can be measured by testing procedures—intelligence, aptitudes, ability to organize, to cope with day-to-day management duties, and to exercise managerial judgment. The centers also measure a candidate's ability to express himself in a group by putting him into an active discussion group. They also attempt to give him practice in coping with real-life situations under some pressure. The main thrust is to place the candidate in a situation that is artificially created to resemble, as closely as possible, an actual situation in an executive job. But this specific technique is, in my opinion, too artificial. The candidate who is called on to make judgment decisions knows that they are only "in play" and that it is not his or his firm's million dollars with which he is playing. Therefore, while there is some measure of his intellectual abilities, there is no real test of his decision-making ability because his decisions are not made under real stress.

The most critical weaknesses of the assessment center approach, however, are these: (1) it does not adequately emphasize measures of decisiveness and courage, and (2) it does not provide for assessing the capacities or the criteria of those who rate the candidates. The seriousness of these failings should be evident in light of the preceding discussion on the failings of raters in general.

These two deficiencies of the assessment center approach are overcome to a large extent in the procedure used in the so-called Patterned Merit Review technique. By this technique, comprehensive assessments on each candidate are obtained from two or more of his bosses under rigidly controlled conditions.

The procedure has several unique advantages. For one thing, the candidate does not participate actively in the assessment; he may not even know he is being evaluated. Hence there is no obligation to show him the results of the assessment—an important point in that the results may be personally disturbing to a candidate who cannot face up to his own weaknesses. Even more important, if the assessor knows that his evaluations are to be reported to the candidate, he is likely to pull his punches and omit truly critical statements.

Another distinctive advantage of the technique is that the ratings are obtained by an interviewer who questions the raters, not the candidate, and keeps them on the track. If the rater is obviously biased, or if he does not know the candidate, the interview is discontinued. The interviewer watches for inconsistencies and simultaneously evaluates the worth of each rater's contribution as he questions him about the candidate.

Since the interviewer must be equal or superior to each rater in rank and status, he feels no hesitation in pointing out any inconsistencies or biases he may note in the rater's comments. Obviously, he needs considerable expertise and psychological insight in preparing the final comprehensive report of his findings; ideally, he should be trained in psychology and psychiatry and be familiar with business mores and practices. These appraisals are then supplemented by in-depth Patterned Interviews.[1]

With the balanced information that can be secured through the three foregoing techniques, a Maverick Executive for the first time will be able to identify staff members with hidden potential or those with hidden weaknesses masked either by a charming personality or by the fact that they have never been subjected to a real test. No appraisal and evaluation process, regardless of its depth and sophistication, is wholly reliable as a predictor of success; however, such techniques are surprisingly useful as predictors of *failure*, since most of the weaknesses revealed (acute anxiety, for example) are of such a nature that the grounds for failure are self-evident.

On the basis of truly reliable tests and in-depth appraisals a Maverick Executive would, at long last, have a truly realistic picture of his management or-

[1] For detailed discussions of the rationale, uses, and interpretation of the Patterned Interview technique, see *Tested Techniques of Personnel Selection* by Robert N. McMurry (Chicago: Dartnell Corp., 1966). Also see *How to Build a Dynamic Sales Organization* (New York: McGraw-Hill, 1968) by Robert N. McMurry and James S. Arnold.

ganization. He could prepare a color-coded "beehive" organization chart that would reveal the superficiality and inaccuracy of his formal organization chart. With a three-dimensional, sociometric chart, he could see his *informal* organization and its channels of communication and could detect the compatibility and incompatibility of executives who often appear as equals on the orthodox organization chart. He could identify the people who have reached their level of incompetence and are currently over their heads, provide back-up men for others, and estimate the executive manpower requirements both currently and for the future.[2]

Unfortunately, the Maverick Executive is not at all likely to undertake voluntarily any comprehensive appraisal of his subordinates. Very few chief executives, in fact, are able to take on such a challenging task; most of them are just too fearful of what they might find. The Maverick Executive is not afraid; his insensitivity to people and his tremendous self-confidence and optimism combine to keep him unaware of the risks generated by misplaced, incompatible, anxiety-ridden personnel. He does not worry about the personal condition of his subordinates; on the contrary, he expects them to do the jobs they are being paid to do. The Maverick Executive believes that if a failing executive can't be "straightened out" with some frank (benevolently autocratic) talk and a stern

[2] For a description and illustration of the beehive chart, see *Clear Communications for Chief Executives* by Robert N. McMurry (*Harvard Business Review*, March–April 1965).

warning or two, then the only thing to do is to replace him with someone who will do what is required.

The Maverick Executive's blindness about the need for accurately appraising his subordinates is fully matched by his ignorance concerning the state of communications in his organization. His concentration on the operations and results of his organization makes him oblivious to the needs of its communications network. He may be irritated by some foul-up in the information he gives out or is given, but he does not regard this as a sign of serious trouble which ought to be corrected. Paradoxically, he himself is adept at protecting his own sources of information and at the same time clumsy enough to damage or inhibit the flow of information from his subordinates.

In his view, information about his plans and the reasons behind his decisions are strictly confidential and are rarely to be shared with even his closest associates. He treats as his private property facts about the company that he regards as critical, and he is extremely cautious about releasing information to the public. His motives seem quite reasonable to him: any fact that might be interpreted as bad news should be withheld because it could damage the company's standing in the stock market. He is unaware that really bad news cannot be withheld—some leakage eventually takes place, with results that are likely to be worse than if the information had been given out promptly. But the Maverick Executive continues to refuse to comment on company problems in the hope that they will not be noticed.

At the same time, the Maverick Executive exhibits

a rather naive faith in his own powers of communication. His self-confidence in his own grasp of a situation leads him to write messages to employees that resound in optimistic generalities and carefully avoid anything that might indicate problems or threatening miscalculations. He does not see that others will not always accept his message on his terms. To be explicit, he is unaware of what is probably the greatest, albeit the least understood, barrier to intracompany communication—a conflict of values that reflects the cultural, educational, and socioeconomic differences between management, on the one hand, and employees under management's control, on the other.

Fully committed to the work ethic, the Maverick Executive sees the bulk of his company's clerical and hourly-rated plant employees in the light of Theory X—that is, as naturally indolent, self-indulgent, and somewhat irresponsible. He feels that workers need discipline and motivation by fear to make them productive. Hence, coercive tactics may be needed to get satisfactory results. Conversely, employees not in management, particularly those at the base of the pyramid, are more pleasure-minded; they live more for today than for tomorrow and are definitely less inclined to subscribe to the work ethic. Their ethic is expressed essentially as "I want to do my own thing and do it in my own way, and I want to do it now because there may not be any tomorrow." Their attitudes toward management—reinforced by the unions acting as "merchants of discontent"—are usually quite negative and include the assumptions that management tends to be greedy, demanding, and exploitative, that it is never to be trusted, and that it willfully withholds pertinent information and distorts the facts. They see themselves as adversaries.

This discrepancy in values forms a communications barrier between the Maverick Executive and his subordinates that not only blocks the acceptance and comprehension of his messages but also blocks or distorts them in transmission. This is because it is difficult, if not almost impossible, for anyone to comprehend, much less accept and assimilate, beliefs and values that are in marked conflict with the ones to which he subscribes. When a message is passed from one person to a second and then on to still others, it is inevitably altered—if not seriously contaminated—by the values of each transmitter. Unmindful of these facts, the Maverick Executive uses first- and second-line supervisors to convey his policy statements to their subordinates; he doesn't realize that these supervisors, though technically they represent management, have risen from the ranks and have values—and antipathies —that are generally consistent with their subordinates'. His messages, therefore, will often be transmitted with a strong bias in favor of labor and against management.

Because he is at the top of his department or his company, a Maverick Executive is, in fact, a prisoner of his position: he receives only the information that his subordinates allow him to receive. Self-protection obviously plays a major role, for all his subordinates are anxious to keep from him any information that might be harmful or discreditable to them. Also, they have learned what he wants to hear and what he would prefer not to hear. Or a subordinate may indulge in self-promotion by putting his competitors in management in a bad light and doing it so skillfully that the Maverick Executive is misled about the qualifications of his subordinates. He is also easily deceived by the workings of an informal conspiracy that calls for silence regarding anything that would change relationships within a group. Troubles and complaints are kept from him; weaknesses and errors of the group's members are covered up. He may be the victim (and properly so, according to their code) of deception, distortion, and other kinds of false information that will protect the security of the group.

In one situation that came to my attention, the billing department of a major railroad somehow neglected to charge a shipper $20,000 for freight services rendered. The executive vice president, as soon as he heard about it, launched an intensive investigation that shook up quite a few people in middle management. In spite of all the uproar, I learned that the president, a Maverick Executive, knew nothing about the matter. The whole affair had been carefully concealed from him by his executive vice president.

All these obstacles to communication are very real, but for a Maverick Executive they do not exist. He sees and hears only what he is primarily interested in. Because he does not recognize the psychological realities of his organization, he is reluctant to take the steps required to improve the flow of information between himself and his subordinates. The first step would be to acknowledge the hard facts about the obstacles preventing good communication. If he could acknowledge the facts, he would discover that he is not universally loved, that he cannot expect his subordinates to behave as he would ideally want them to. But it would take him years to develop the kind of subjective honesty and self-perception that would allow him to face the anxieties, disloyalties, bitter rivalries, vengefulness, and other weaknesses of his subordinates that are crippling communications.

Nor can the Maverick Executive be expected to take the second step toward improving communications in his organization, which would be to undertake a comprehensive and extended program of objectively appraising every member of his management and supervisory staff in the way that was outlined earlier. Finally, he is not disposed to take the third step, which is to establish a system for finding out what the employees like and dislike about their jobs and what their beliefs and values are.

Does this mean that nothing can be done to improve communications in an organization led by a Maverick Executive? One answer is that nothing can be done if the Maverick Executive is so dominant that he brooks no interference with his management of the company. All too often this is the case. However, it is possible to improve communications in the company if the board of directors or a very large stockholder has enough leverage with the Maverick Executive to persuade him to go along with one or more of the steps cited above.

The chances are very slim that a Maverick Executive will agree to try to sharpen his self-perceptions and his understanding of how other people behave in his organization. He may, through reading and discussions with other executives, improve his talents for listening and for asking the right questions, but his basic nature will in all probability continue to impair his powers of communicating with others. On the other hand, his lack of empathy may even help him accept the other two programs—an in-depth appraisal of his subordinates and an accurate, controlled survey of employee attitudes and opinions. Most chief executives lack the courage to face the hard truths about the people working under them, but the Maverick Executive is never short on courage and, where people are concerned, sees nothing to be afraid of. He may think these measures are unnecessary and he cannot be counted on to advocate them. Nevertheless, if they can be undertaken without his opposition, the Maverick Executive may begin to see that his ways of managing information have limitations.

Nothing will educate him faster than a really accurate, penetrating employee opinion poll. To find out what employees actually think about their jobs and to learn their values, a survey is needed of the entire spectrum of opinions, ideas, grievances, ideologies, and resentments to be found among the nonmanagerial personnel. Securing an objective report on these attitudes is no easy task, for employees usually resent management's probing into their opinions and behaviors and are very suspicious of any such attempts. They are aware that too often in the past management has used this kind of information to identify the employees it wishes to remove from the payroll or discipline in some other way.

The fear of management reprisals is so pervasive that employees do not tell the truth unless they are absolutely sure they won't be identified. Therefore, most polls of employee attitudes are largely a useless collection of carefully screened opinions and statements designed to tell management what employees think it wants to hear. Whatever information is obtained is generally biased on the favorable side, since favorable responses beget no reprisals. To reassure employees that their identities will be hidden and secure their acceptance of the poll as a valid and honest effort to get at the truth, several precautions must be taken.

Since personnel departments are frequently regarded as management's stool pigeons, a first precaution is to engage an independent, outside agency to conduct the poll. The size of the units to be polled should be determined, and any supervisor's group of fewer than ten people should be consolidated with other small groups into a single unit to encourage employees to believe that their individual identities will be protected. Next, after the employees have had the rationale of the poll explained to them (preferably by a senior executive) copies of a simple, multiple-choice questionnaire of 25 to 30 items are placed in a pile and each employee is invited to select at random the blank he or she will complete; this precludes the possibility of any individual's being identified by some secret system of marking or keying on the questionnaires. Separate series of questions are used for each division, category, or level of work in order to adapt them to intracompany conditions.

All questions can be answered with a check mark and no employee is asked to sign his name or provide identifying data of any kind. As a further precaution, it may be necessary to muzzle in advance, by threats of immediate dismissal, any supervisor who may be inclined to intimidate his people by implying that he has arcane techniques that will enable him to know what an employee has said.

With all the foregoing assurances, usually 85 to 90 percent of employees polled speak up clearly and frankly. Only 10 to 15 percent will still be too fearful to state honestly what they feel and think, and will usually give unrealistically favorable answers.

In the second stage of this polling procedure, employees are told that management would like to have the polling agency interview 10 to 15 percent of the personnel to find out about any conditions or grievances not covered by the questionnaire. Each employee is asked to write on 3" by 5" cards the names of any three other employees (but not supervisors) who are familiar with the group's needs and problems and to drop these cards into the ballot boxes with their questionnaires. The names of these nominees are then posted (a minimum of five per unit) and employees are asked to give them their additional comments and opinions.

These nominees are usually the natural leaders of each unit, and their opinions yield the really significant information obtained in the survey: they provide the qualitative information as to *why* morale is good or poor. They may reveal some facts about specific issues such as polluted drinking water, excessive temperatures, inadequate lockers, and favoritism exhibited by supervisors. The nominees report only on why they think their fellow employees like, dislike, or need things, never on their own likes, dislikes, or needs, thereby protecting themselves from reprisals. A specific grievance is not important unless it is stressed by several or all of these leaders.

Furthermore, these leaders can be used as sounding boards for management's ideas in proposed communications. From their reactions, management can quickly determine whether a message is consistent with employee values and is understood and accepted by them. If they do not understand or accept it, management can take steps to reformulate the message to make it acceptable.

To a Maverick Executive, the benefits of such an employee polling program will be limited to those that contribute directly to the company's performance. Improvements in communications between people and departments are in his view desirable only when some specific information reveals a problem that calls for management action. Then the Maverick Executive will act, often in situations where other chief executives will hesitate or back off. For example, employee grievances that depress morale are often the result of traditional company practices—shutting down a plant for summer vacations, for instance, may greatly annoy many employees but may be continued year after year because of precedent or because it suits management's convenience. A Maverick Executive, on learning of the employees' dissatisfaction, would find out whether the practice contributed to the plant's profit margins; if it did, he would decide in favor of the practice and against the employees. There would be no failure of communication in his opinion but rather a successful discovery of information needed for a correct decision.

To the Maverick Executive, good communication generally means letting his subordinates know unmistakably that he intends to keep the company healthy and growing, no matter what. In the case of one company, a thorough appraisal of management, made with the approval of the Maverick Executive, revealed a considerable number of incompetent supervisors. The executive ordered an extensive housecleaning that promptly cleared them out. This inevitably produced anxiety in many employees. Typically, the Maverick Executive did not try to smooth things over; instead, he frankly said, in effect, "If you survived this shake-up, your job is reasonably safe." The survivors, knowing that the ordeal was over, felt relieved.

Decisive action of this kind involves difficult and unpleasant decisions for most chief executives. Many therefore continue to substitute wishful thinking for action. They may believe, for instance, that good communications and good morale depend on compatibility and that it is important to retain even incompetent subordinates who are compatible. The Maverick Executive makes no such mistake; he insists on having compatible subordinates, and separating a compatible but incompetent subordinate from the company is not difficult for him. It is an intelligent, necessary act. Ironically, though it probably doesn't occur to him, by such an act he can improve both communications and morale since his staff, at least, will be even more careful not to misinform him and will also be increasingly proud of the stress he places on their competence.

HOW TO FIND
AND LIVE WITH A
MAVERICK EXECUTIVE

6

No matter how successful a company may become under the driving leadership of a Maverick Executive, it will almost inevitably develop two great internal weaknesses: there will be very few strong, independent managers in its ranks, and not a single top executive will be competent to take over the No. 1 post in case the Maverick Executive dies or leaves. Nevertheless, the appeal and performance of the Maverick Executive are such that these penalties are widely ignored. His own directors rarely realize either the debilitating effect he has on his subordinates or that he will be reluctant to develop a strong successor. Other directors who may seek a Maverick Executive to invigorate their companies are not likely to know the first thing about where or how to find one or how to handle one they have hired.

The fact is that not every enterprise developed by a Maverick Executive needs another one to administer it as his successor; there are times when a conservative executive is needed to consolidate the gains and growth inaugurated by his predecessor. But where a Maverick Executive does seem called for—and only an assessment of a company's growth cycle, competition, markets, products, services, and other factors can determine this—then the attitudes and practices of this breed of executive become exceedingly important.

For one thing, a Maverick Executive gives no more than passing attention to what every really competent executive considers the most important single responsibility of management: that is, the selection and development of executives. His enormous self-confidence, his strong ego and will to succeed, his distrust of others, and his lack of empathy all combine to make him oblivious to the need for strong subordinates. And his drive to gain and hold the top power position makes him unable to tolerate any subordinate who is potentially able to challenge him and eventually take over his job. Moreover, in his perennial optimism he is overconfident that *his* organization, built and guided by his own hand, will continue to be ahead of its competitors for years and years, and he cannot visualize himself as dying or even retiring. To him, having a strong No. 2 man as a potential successor is not only unnecessary, it is a threatening reflection on *his* capacity.

For all these reasons, the Maverick Executive is at the same time very poorly equipped to choose and develop able subordinates. As a result, this crucial task usually remains neglected unless or until some concerned directors or stockholders press the issue. Ordinarily this does not happen until the Maverick

Executive is ready to—or obliged to—step down. And then the directors face an assignment which theoretically they are legally responsible for, but which they are actually often the least qualified to perform.

There are several reasons for this. First and foremost, a director's success in his own business or field does not by any means qualify him as a good judge of men. Indeed, some are abominably poor as executives and very superficial in assessing managers; few are aware that if an executive is to be successful in the top position he must possess a special mix of traits, qualities, and motivations. Most of them tend to be positive thinkers, focusing their attention simplistically on what they assume to be the candidate's best qualities and capacities: he is a "sound thinker, good administrator, technically brilliant," and so on. They have conspicuously little interest in finding out weaknesses. This lopsidedness, more than any other factor, accounts for the large number of incredible, egregious blunders made by directors and other executives in picking top leaders for companies they are expected to supervise.

The blunders will be multiplied and intensified when directors are looking for a Maverick Executive to head their company. The first essential, therefore, in beginning such a search is to know what the most common errors are. Perhaps the worst mistake is to take the word of the retiring chief executive that his close associate, the No. 2 man, will be able to qualify for the No. 1 spot. A dynamic chief executive with an outstanding record sometimes seeks a conservator to succeed him and maintain his traditions and policies relatively unchanged. But a second-place subordinate, serving in a complementary way to the chief executive, is rarely a leader in his own right. He may be able to emulate a Maverick Executive by being very skillful in achieving organizational harmony through political stratagems and conniving; however, without the Maverick Executive's other capacities, particularly his drive and decisiveness, this kind of politicking does not make for long-term success.

Another serious error is to assume that a son of the chief executive or some other relative will qualify. Nepotism is rarely a successful practice and is especially hazardous for a Maverick Executive. Such individuals often have weak sons who prove the old adage, "From shirtsleeves to shirtsleeves in three generations." On the other hand, it is just as great a mistake to place strong emphasis on specialized competence. The selection of a specialist for the top job is usually the result of some temporary fad or shortage. The emphasis on computer technology, for example, has installed more than one specialist as a chief executive whose poor overall judgment and lack of real organizing and administrative ability brought disaster to their companies.

The search for a Maverick Executive, however, is most often defeated by the mistakes of simple ignorance. Directors, no more than chief executives, simply do not know what specific personal qualities and capacities are required for success as a Maverick Executive. Some favor a candidate who "looks like a president." Others favor a man who looks something like themselves. (The executive who picks a subordinate in his own image has become a cliché in modern management, but directors do this too.) Some chief executives have been selected mainly because they happen to be compatible or socially well connected with some directors or top officers of the company. Wishful thinking credits the candidate with qualities he does not have; he may be extremely positive and assert with great self-confidence that he can handle the job, and his technical skill and experience may be convincing, yet he may be totally lacking in the essentials of a Maverick Executive.

The Maverick Executive himself is living proof of how defective are the criteria that are normally used to find him, for his qualities are almost exactly the opposite of those that would make him popular with directors and senior officers. He is the polar opposite of the Organization Man and is entirely lacking in caution, docility, and conformity, the qualities that would make him a loyal member of the team. He tends to be extremely demanding, ruthless, and generally disagreeable. Frequently he is somewhat of a conniver, a politician aiming for power. He is impatient and unwilling to advance by seniority. He wants to get to the top as fast as possible and throughout his career he has not remained more than two or three years on the same job. On the way up he was generally disliked by his superiors because of his nonconformity and outspokenness; he may have been reported as insolent, argumentative, and even arrogant, especially for his criticism of company policies and his bosses' decisions.

His behavior has never been readily predictable.

He is apt to take off on a tangent when a fresh idea strikes him. He is apt to believe, and rightly so, that he is more competent than his bosses, so that he often behaves in an insubordinate way, sometimes overtly, more often covertly. He is not only reluctant to support any of his bosses' rulings with which he disagrees —he openly criticizes them to his own subordinates. He may have quit a job or jobs that dissatisfied him and even been very active in union affairs. In fact, his sympathies are more often, logically and rationally, with his subordinates and their problems even though he does not feel close to them.

It is not surprising, therefore, that potential Maverick Executives are seldom given a chance to grow up through the ranks. Many of them get along so poorly with their bosses that they resign after a short time and do their climbing in other companies; they are "mobi-centric"—that is, they change jobs at frequent intervals until they are able to reach the top spot, as Professor Eugene Jennings has well pointed out.[1] Some of them have used their record with a corporation as a springboard, subsequently raising their own capital to start a new company as an entrepreneur.

Clearly, those who are seeking a Maverick Executive for the top job in a company should have in mind the kind of executive who will definitely be a calculated risk. His special mix of characteristics will almost certainly insure his initial nonacceptance by practically all the senior officers and most of the

---

[1] Eugene Emerson Jennings, *Routes to the Executive Suite* (New York: McGraw-Hill, 1971).

others in management. His abrasiveness, insensitivity, and other disagreeable characteristics are part of the price to be paid for the drive, courage, and self-assurance that will keep the company ahead of its competitors.

Assuming that the directors of a company will pay this price and accept the risks in taking a Maverick Executive, they will have to decide which course to follow in order to find their man. They can either look carefully inside the company or go searching for a restless Maverick Executive in another company. The first course is the least promising by far, for it assumes that an executive with the necessary qualifications has also had the atypical patience to endure intermediate jobs, transfers, slow promotions, and the frustrations caused by bureaucrats and autocrats who do their best to block the progress of such an executive up the ladder. Nevertheless, when a company's policy of promotion from within for the sake of morale is very strong, or where there are other impelling internal political reasons, a search for a Maverick Executive within the ranks may be successful. The following precautions, however, should certainly be taken:

1. Avoid one of the commonest errors in seeking candidates for executive posts: do not look for top executive material among those in middle management. This is where administrators flourish, where jobs are so highly structured that managers get almost no experience in decision making and risk taking.

2. Ask everyone who holds a management position to name every candidate he can think of for the post

of chief executive. Then give the candidates a rough screening to exclude all those who are too young (under 35) or too old (over 50), lack varied business training and experience, lack skill in decision making, have shown personality traits or eccentricities that are characteristic of conforming, dependent managers. (See Chapter 7). Beware especially of candidates endorsed by conformist, conservative middle managers who tend to promote only those "good" employees who have such homely virtues as long and faithful service, industriousness, loyalty, and obedience.

3. Appraise the survivors in depth, using the Patterned Merit Review (described in Chapter 5) to identify the ones appearing to have some promise. This appraisal would probably reduce the original group to a remaining 1 to 5 percent. These most promising prospects are then told they are being considered for the top job and asked if they will submit to tests and interviews in an assessment center. Few will refuse.

4. Evaluate the remaining candidates by using assessment center techniques—personal history analysis, performance tests, psychological tests, and a comprehensive patterned interview.

5. Subject the most promising candidates to trial in the field. The assignment must be relatively unstructured and very demanding. For example, one international company, which has a 50 percent interest in a Brazilian manufacturing concern, sends a candidate to work in Brazil with the two Brazilian partners who own the other half interest. There, 3,000 miles from the home office, he must cope with a foreign language,

a volatile economy, an unstable political situation, and a pair of partners who, though politically well connected, are so untrustworthy they are known in the New York headquarters as the "two burglars." Under these conditions he is expected not only to protect the company's interests but to make decisions that will return to the company a profit on the operation.

It is a final trial by fire of this kind that provides the ultimate test of a candidate's capacity to endure and succeed under brutal conditions. Many bright and capable men will fail such a test, but the Maverick Executive will enthusiastically welcome the challenges and risks involved and will think up smart, new ways of coming out ahead. He may commit some fairly big boners in the process, but he will further prove what he is by his powers of recovery. The virtues of severe testing on the job have been described by Antony Jay: "Men grow to the stature to which they are stretched when they are young; and the ones who are not stretched will fail to grow; some will actually be diminished." [2]

However, the chances of finding a Maverick Executive inside the company are always very slim. Having subjected the candidates to all the steps in this process, it is most likely to be discovered that not even the most promising one is a Maverick Executive. In that case, the search will have to be continued outside the company.

Looking for a Maverick Executive in other companies involves even more obstacles than are met in

[2] *Management and Machiavelli*, p. 65.

an intracompany search. To begin with, a Maverick Executive outside the ranks is a total unknown; his background, record, personality, and strengths and weaknesses will therefore have to be investigated with great thoroughness. Locating even a few candidates will be a time-consuming, frustrating, and costly operation. Finally, every candidate will undoubtedly be as suspicious of his interviewers as they are of him; unlike a Maverick Executive in the company, he has no company loyalty and is not motivated to win a big promotion; he seeks to "make it big by himself."

To meet these and other obstacles to finding a Maverick Executive who might be pirated from another organization, the following steps are recommended:

1. Check the records of all managers who have quit the company in recent years. One of them may be a genuine maverick who resigned because his insecure boss, resenting his brash and independent ways, choked off his ideas, curtailed his authority, and refused to recommend him for promotion. If these actual causes of his quitting can be verified by his former colleagues, then a follow-up on such a manager may produce a promising candidate.

2. Avoid the practice of acquiring a small company in order to acquire the talents of its chief executive or one of his young tigers. This has been widely regarded as a prime technique for getting top executive timber. However, such a prize candidate as a Maverick Executive is practically never snared this way. The reason is that a high proportion of companies taken over are already sick, having been badly man-

aged by poorly qualified executives; any Maverick Executives would long since have moved elsewhere.

3. Use the usual tested sources—knowledgeable business and professional people and carefully placed advertisements—to secure recommended candidates. Since the Maverick Executive's complex mix of characteristics and capacities is still so little known, probably none of these suggested candidates will qualify. However, in order to find one who does possess the proper mix, it may be necessary to consider, to some degree, a minimum of a hundred candidates, and every source should be tapped.

4. Locate an executive recruiting firm that knows how to look for hard-to-find candidates. Ask several firms to describe their methods. At a minimum, these should include two essential preliminary steps: first, the recruiter must ascertain *all* the requirements of the top job, with special attention to the degree of control planned by the directors—or by the retiring chief executive if the Maverick Executive is to begin working under him. Second, the recruiter must study the executives over whom the Maverick Executive will be working to see how compatible—or incompatible—they will be with him. Only after these two tasks are completed should the recruiter start seeking candidates who will measure up to the specified criteria.

Specifying the dimensions of the job a Maverick Executive will be asked to take over has to be done far more carefully than would be the case when seeking other kinds of executives. A Maverick Executive will ask very hard questions about the company, particularly about the assurance of being in complete control. The company's stance in its markets, its competitive position, its financial condition—especially its capacity to underwrite new projects—the competence of its management staff, the influence of outside directors and large stockholders, all these should be thoroughly explored by a recruiter before he attempts to outline the specifics of the top job. Once that has been done, he can turn to searching for those rare candidates who might be available.

The process of screening a large number of candidates to eliminate the unqualified can be speeded up by using a series of knockout questions. Some of the questions—for example, "Why would you like to be president of this company?"—are aimed to ascertain the candidate's real interest in the position, his life goals and his aspirations. If he exhibits intense interest in the financial compensation and perquisites of the job, if he likes the idea of being thought of as a great leader of a large organization, he is probably not a good candidate. These things are, of course, of interest to a Maverick Executive, but he will take them for granted.

Other questions would concern the candidate's values as they relate to the job, the industry, and business in general. He may, for example, be biased against certain business practices and the products of a particular industry. The attitudes of a Maverick Executive will usually be flexible, unless they are based on the work ethic, in which case he will rigidly abide by his convictions. Similarly, questioning the candidate about his management ideas can be very revealing. What does he think about delegating authority to subordinates or asking for their opinions and recommendations on decisive issues? Most candidates will either freely approve these ideas or cautiously hedge their answers to avoid confrontation with the views of a future employer. Indeed, under pressure of these knockout questions, most candidates will tend to give answers they think will be acceptable to the recruiter or whoever else may be interviewing them. But a Maverick Executive has no fear of expressing himself with great openness and frankness, even at the risk of offending his interviewer.

The process of questioning candidates is as much a test of the interviewer as it is of the interviewee. It has to be done subtly in ways that, on the one hand, will indicate clearly what kind of man the company is looking for and, on the other, will not induce a candidate to falsify his real attitudes and feelings. Even an outspoken Maverick Executive will know that his values may sound too radical to the interviewer, and will temper his answers if he likes the challenge of the job and senses that his full credo may be too strong for those connected with the company. Also, his great self-confidence and abounding optimism will tend to exaggerate his replies to some questions, such as how soon he feels he can put the company in front of its competitors.

The sincerity of each candidate's responses must therefore be carefully tested. This may be done by checking his judgments against the judgments of those who are presumably more objective. A former associate, perhaps, or an old friend will probably recognize characteristic exaggerations, self-promoting statements, and purposely ambiguous replies. At the same time, however, it is always more than possible that a Maverick Executive will actually be able to accomplish all the things he may confidently predict. The uncertainty of this simply has to be accepted as part of the risk of acquiring a Maverick Executive.

Once a candidate has answered the knockout questions to the recruiter's satisfaction, he should then be examined in depth for the specific capacities he would need in handling the particular problems and situations facing the company. The crucial aspect of this appraisal is never the evaluation of the candidate's technical competence and experience. These are not primarily relevant, because a Maverick Executive's success does not depend on them; in fact, his technical know-how and past experiences may have little to do with the company's requirements. He is an extraordinary, highly intelligent generalist who can swiftly learn all he needs to know to run any business. What an appraiser should look for in a candidate are sure evidences of those key traits that generally mark the Maverick Executive—tremendous self-confidence, drive, and decisiveness—along with all those other characteristic traits that comprise his make-up: optimism, nonconformity, lack of empathy, impatience, and so forth. While psychological testing and a depth interview will confirm the existence of many of these characteristics, others may have to be inferred from data and incidents reported by businessmen and personal friends.

Since even highly qualified conservative chief executives are in very short supply, finding candidates with Maverick Executive potentials is often extremely difficult, time consuming, costly, and frustrating. The task may take from six months to a year or longer, and may involve $50,000 or more in direct costs. However, the search may be speeded up if the seekers are Maverick Executives themselves or are very experienced in dealing with such men. A good example was provided by Columbia Broadcasting System's Board Chairman William S. Paley and Vice Chairman Frank Stanton. Eight months after having recruited and installed Charles T. Ireland, Jr. (then senior vice president of I.T.T.), as president of CBS, they had to do the job all over again when Mr. Ireland died suddenly. Within the very short space of a month, they made their choice: Arthur Robert Taylor, a 37-year-old with an M.A. in American economic history and only 11 years' experience in the business world, none of it in the broadcasting industry.

However, Taylor's background, educational achievements, and ambitions display a great many of the characteristic marks of a potential Maverick Executive. According to newspaper accounts,[3] Taylor, who grew up in Rahway, New Jersey, said, "If you could survive the experience of going to high school there, you were a pretty tough nut." Of his graduating classmates, two went to college and ten went to Sing Sing. At 12, he began working at odd jobs and he earned his support through college by working as a hardware store clerk, a cutter in a cheese factory, and a shirt salesman. His drive for success was intense. As

[3] *The New York Times,* July 13 and July 16, 1972.

115

one of his high school friends commented, "He's always had this phenomenal drive. He said he was going to conduct the All-State Orchestra, and he did. He said he was going after the state oratory contest, and he won it. Then he won the biggest scholarship to Brown." He graduated from there magna cum laude with a Phi Beta Kappa key and immediately became an admissions officer at Brown and later an assistant director as well as a proctor in a dormitory.

In 1961, when he received his master's degree, he intended to enter the teaching profession; instead, he took a job as a trainee at the First Boston Corporation. In three years he was an assistant vice president; in five, a vice president in the underwriting department; and by 1969, a director of the corporation and responsible for developing new business. The next year he was plucked by International Paper Company to be its financial vice president.

Taylor's former colleagues have described his executive qualities:

> He's a pushy guy—extremely bright and ambitious—but there's something else, a magnetism he has that makes people very confident of what he has to say. Partly he's a con man. . . . He's a brilliant, restless, fantastically hard-working, hard-bargaining, driven sort of guy, not the sort you'd think of as an investment banker, a guy capable of rubbing people the wrong way under pressure, but who usually takes a cool, analytical, and even intellectual approach to his work.

Typically, Taylor exhibited his extreme independence when, as a college freshman, he was interviewing campus politicians for a local radio station and the station manager, disliking the people and issues he was introducing, wanted to approve them in advance. "I had heard about freedom of the press since I was fifteen," Taylor said, "so I walked out in a huff." Not so typical of a Maverick Executive are Taylor's objective view of himself ("People either like me or they don't.") and his salesmanship ("It's true that I have the ability to persuade, which is a verbal activity and has played a strong role. But I do have points of view, and I encourage dissent.").

Taylor's business philosophy also helped to qualify him for the presidency of CBS. He believes that a corporation can discharge its responsibility to society only by becoming profitable, a view that is entirely compatible with Paley's determination to diversify CBS. In the opinion of Vice Chairman Stanton, Taylor is "the right man at the right age and stage of business development to take the responsibility of the presidency of the company."

There is, of course, no guarantee that Taylor will remain with CBS to become its chief executive officer when Mr. Paley retires. If he should begin to feel incompatible with the men above him, he would most likely leave. While he appears to have most of the traits that mark a Maverick Executive, it remains to be seen whether or not he has them all and finally decides that CBS is the most rewarding place for him to work.

The uncertainty that surrounds any Maverick Executive is a crucial factor that directors simply have to cope with. It cannot be assumed that the organization is going to be perfectly safe in his hands. For one thing, his tendency to overoptimism can put the company deep in the red on some ventures and unexpectedly in the black on others. And his insensitivity to people and frequent abrasiveness will undoubtedly rile many of his subordinates and drive some to resign rather than endure his autocratic control. If there is a potential Maverick Executive in the company, he will eventually leave. And neither executive development programs nor committee meetings will get much attention from the maverick chief, which will inevitably make it difficult both to recruit and to retain the most ambitious and promising young managers.

Moreover, a Maverick Executive is not going to develop any successor who could possibly challenge his hold on the top position. Yet he may shrewdly motivate his close subordinates by giving them the impression that he would choose one of them as his eventual successor. One company president whom I observed made it a common practice to pit his executive committee members against each other by hinting that one of the five was to be his successor. But he never made it clear which one he had in mind, and just before he retired he brought in his successor from outside the company.

Of all the Maverick Executive's weaknesses this failure to groom a strong successor is certainly the most ominous for the company's future. But this seems to be an incurable blindspot of great achievers; there are extremely few examples in history or in industry of great leaders having chosen and developed great successors. From this standpoint, the decision to seek a Maverick Executive for the top post of a company must be regarded as a short-term strategy whose benefits, it is hoped, will outweigh the penalties.

There are, however, several precautions that directors can take to protect the company and themselves against those penalties. Before the Maverick Executive has been installed, the board can firm up its overall constraints on the chief executive's operations. A major control to be strengthened is the finance committee composed of directors who oversee and review major expenditures of the corporation. Specific ceilings can be placed on the Maverick Executive's authority to commit the company's funds, for example, although such ceilings would have to be fairly generous to interest a Maverick Executive in the first place. Another powerful control is an executive committee composed of key executives who, in the opinion of the outside directors, are most genuinely interested in the company's welfare: through such a committee the board can develop its own sources of intracompany intelligence that will keep tabs on how the Maverick Executive's policies and behavior are affecting the organization. Still another control might be through obligating the company's public accountants to broaden their activities to include more of the controller's functions, such as appraising trends and future risks.

Nevertheless, directors must realize that controls of any kind, except his own, are odious to a Maverick Executive, and he will do everything he can to evade them. Being what he is, he must have freedom to move in new directions, to take risks confidently, to change things drastically, and to place corporate advantage and success ahead of any personal considerations. Directors should also be aware that he will do his best to establish his own system of controls over the board and its committees. Though the odds against his fully succeeding may be great, he tries to develop among them the conviction that they are fulfilling their obligations to play an active role in controlling and reviewing the major decisions of the chief executive.

He does not want the directors to abdicate all their legal responsibilities, for he is mindful of such catastrophes as those that befell the Penn Central Railroad and its officers when its directors totally ignored their responsibilities. A skillful Maverick Executive does all he can to make his directors feel they are participating responsibly; he asks their advice, leaves them to discuss matters alone, and so on. In giving them information about the company's operations and the ways in which he is gaining its objectives, he strives, like all chief executives, to convince them he is following the right course. The difference is that his charisma and super-confidence have the power to dissolve their doubts and cautions and persuade them to depend entirely on his judgment and decisions.

His influence naturally sways those of his subordinates who may be serving as inside directors, but it also prevails even when his board is dominated by outside directors. One Maverick Executive displays his enormous confidence in his persuasive powers by staffing his board almost exclusively with outside directors, several of whom are retirees—former senior executives in banking, accounting, and manufacturing firms. He appears to involve them very actively in the almost day-to-day running of the company, treating them more like consultants than ordinary directors. In advance of each monthly board meeting, he sends out an agenda of topics to be covered, a statement of the company's financial condition, a summary of its sales position, the state of its labor relations, and other relevant information. The assumption is that with such advance intelligence, the company will gain the benefit of its directors' business skills and possible contributions as consultants. The Maverick Executive, however, carefully manages to keep all the major and most of the minor decisions in his own hands.

If a Maverick Executive succeeds in this, if he adroitly persuades his directors that they are discharging their obligations while he actually retains a free hand in decision making and in directing the corporation, then he has completed the final step in demonstrating that he fully deserves the title of Maverick Executive.

HOW HE CONTRIBUTES
TO EXECUTIVE FAILURE

7

One of the most significant shortcomings in a Maverick Executive, one he shares with most other executives, is an almost total lack of a sense of responsibility for executives who fail. Very few chief executives even recognize the obligation. They do accept responsibility for the development and *success* of their subordinates, and they spend considerable sums of money and time in the process, but they are not willing to hold themselves accountable for executives who are *failures*.

It is not surprising, therefore, that a substantial segment of the management population at all levels, especially those in unstructured executive positions, are psychological casualties. In one survey of 2,803 businessmen, nearly 30 percent claimed that job requirements had adversely affected their health at one time or another during the past five years, and that most of their health-related difficulties resulted from increased strain and tension brought on by heightened

day-to-day business pressures.[1] It may even be said
that certain management practices are the direct
(though certainly unintentional) cause of many deaths
and many more physical and emotional breakdowns.
The most common of all such casualties are the overpromoted executives. These are the persons described
by Lawrence Peter as having reached their first levels
of incompetence.[2]

The overpromoted executive is by far the biggest
people problem in management. Most managers, like
all people who work for wages, are dependent; if they
were not, they would be in business for themselves
or in some profession. The overdependent executive,
however, having reached a position requiring decisions he is incapable of making with confidence, feels
threatened, insecure, and inadequate and is emotionally dependent on his superiors. He has become an
almost universal institution, yet overdependence is
rarely mentioned as a problem in management literature. The concept itself is so anxiety producing that
very few executives are willing even to discuss it.
From my own observations, it emerges as the one
topic above all others that executives wish to avoid or
conceal. Indeed, their attitude toward the overdependency problem is comparable to society's treatment of
venereal disease at the turn of the century: If it isn't
discussed, it doesn't exist.

[1] Dale Tranowieski, *The Changing Success Ethic* (New
York: Amacom, 1973), p. 2.
[2] Lawrence J. Peter and Raymond Hull, *The Peter Principle* (New York: William Morrow, 1969).

The Maverick Executive is no more willing or able than other executives to discuss this overdependency problem, but he differs from them in two respects. First, other executives have a latent but rarely expressed fear that they themselves may be somewhat overdependent. But the Maverick Executive has no such fear—his ego is simply too healthy and aggressive, and his successes have continuously increased his self-confidence. In the second place, he simply cannot tolerate strong, independent subordinates. He is so accustomed to wielding absolute power that he accepts no rivals. He subscribes to the old barnyard maxim: "There is room for only one bull in the pasture."

At the same time, however, there are many other reasons why a Maverick Executive does not accept responsibility for the proliferation of overdependent executives among his subordinates. To a large extent, his reasons are primarily rationalizations and represent the psychological, economic, and social errors common to almost all executives. These mistakes are so varied and numerous that only the major ones can be considered here.

1. He steadily and simplistically maintains that every man is responsible solely for himself and that if an executive fails, he alone should bear the consequences of his "inadequacies." This stern insistence on individualism ignores not only all the psychological and social factors involved in any failure, but also all those errors repeatedly committed by management in its selection, appraisal, and placement of personnel.

2. The Maverick Executive accepts the management myth that if a man has been successful in one management position or at one level in the hierarchy, he must be, ipso facto, a person of stature, superior competence, self-confidence, and inherent managerial ability and is therefore capable of success at a higher level.

The truth is that an executive who does an excellent job in a highly structured, routinized, and regimented position, where he has no significant decisions to make and has no supervisory responsibilities, is apt to be in serious trouble when he is advanced to a position in which he has only minimal guidance and support. He may be intelligent and well educated, he may have long experience and marvelous intentions, but if he is unable to cope with problems and make decisions by himself, he is almost certain to fail.

3. The Maverick Executive, lacking knowledge of people, is likely to place potentially threatened executives in line, decision-making, supervisory positions. Like most of the executives who are responsible for promotions in management, the Maverick normally has only an elementary conception of the basic requirements for success in such positions. He does not even know how to begin to evaluate a candidate's qualifications for such responsibilities; as pointed out in Chapter 5, he does not know the differences in the psychological demands of line and staff positions, he depends on superficial and obvious criteria and the time-worn factors of technical competence, loyalty, schooling, and length of service. Though he himself has the essentials, he does not realize that self-reliance

and risk-taking capacities are indispensable for success at higher levels of line management.

4. The Maverick Executive, like many top management executives, is likely to promote on an informal, irrational basis. In some cases he will advance the only man proposed by his boss—often frankly described as the "best of the worst." In other cases, personal favoritism or intracompany politics decides his choice; or he may kick some inconvenient—if not yet potential—rival upstairs to get him out of the way.

5. A Maverick Executive may resort to the Procrustean bed technique for fitting overqualified and underqualified executives into jobs. An overqualified executive may be openly denigrated. One Maverick, for example, referred to such a man as "too smart-ass for his own good." An underqualified executive may be quietly buried, placed in a dead-end job where he is expected to abide in solitude; or he may be subjected to endless programs of training and "self-development," which the Maverick Executive considers valueless but which can keep the man out of his hair.

Basically, all these malpractices in placing executives occur because the Maverick Executive has not established reasonable criteria of performance and a valid technology for assessing his subordinates. But he also regularly contributes directly and insidiously to the dependence of his subordinates. Because he is authoritarian and makes all the key decisions, no one on his staff is likely to develop the capacity for making decisions independently. Moreover, because he is temperamentally incapable of delegating authority, he accentuates the dependence of his subordinates by making their decisions for them.

Even those who initially might have shown some independence he readily seduces into a state of comfortable and complacent acquiescence. A few stern threats thrown in with some ample rewards for compliance usually suffice; after all, as every employee knows, no one ever got fired by the boss for following his instructions. Within a short time, the Maverick Executive surrounds himself with a coterie of Little Sir Echoes.

Ironically, the Maverick Executive does not see that he himself is to blame for indecisive subordinates and so he feels free to belittle them to outsiders. One 60-year-old Maverick president who consulted me referred, in fact, to his executive colleagues as cringing wretches who feared to express themselves in any way. Another, who is the president of a $50 million family-owned company, told me that his executives "refuse ever to make even the slightest decision, bucking every question to me, no matter how trivial." He had not overtly castrated his subordinates; he simply had no confidence in their judgment and did not hesitate to voice this opinion, expecting to convince others that no one but himself had the answers. In one unfortunate sense he was right. By a process of his own selection, no one with leadership quality remained with him. (He was also typically sure he would live forever and hence needed no successor.)

Despite the Maverick Executive's scorn for his submissive and compliant subordinates, he would not have it any other way. Indeed, he has his particular reasons for preferring docile and dependent executives. Not only are they never a threat to his total authority, but they are basically more dependable and predictable because their security is at stake. As a rule, the over-dependent executive is an excellent craftsman in his specialty, and the Maverick Executive relies on him for that almost exclusively.

Actually, as the Maverick Executive is well aware, these technically competent but inherently anxious organization men are industry's indispensables. They are the ones who see to it that the routines somehow get carried out on a day-to-day basis. Hence they are regarded by the Maverick Executive (and by most other executives) as ideal for first-, second-, or third-line supervision. Indeed, they usually meet all the common criteria for the "ideal" supervisor: They are faithful, loyal (at least superficially), technically competent, usually have long service records, and pose no threat to their bosses.

Unfortunately, these criteria are also often assumed to be essential for success in an executive post (although some are even counterindications) and the result is a promotion that produces an insecure executive. Without the capacities of self-reliance and courage in risk taking, such an executive is like an excellent first violinist who, though unqualified as an orchestra conductor, has nevertheless been promoted to that position. In every company the ranks of supervision are loaded with managers who are over their heads in their jobs, who should never have been trusted with the responsibilities of decision-making line management. The best place for such employees is in subordinate staff positions where they can "hew the wood and carry the water" in their companies. Among them are the clerks with titles who have accumulated 40 or 50 years of seniority, the career salesmen who form the backbone of every distribution system, and the senior skilled technicians without whose know-how a factory cannot operate efficiently.

The Maverick Executive knows that without such subordinates he could not run his company. And because they are normally docile and dependable, he also appreciates them for helping to give him the kind of company he most admires, a company where peace and harmony appear to reign and where strife is avoided at all costs. In his opinion, only an enterprise that is completely free from conflict internally can be truly "a team." (He would not use a fancy term like synergistic.) Other executives may see this state as one close to the repose of death, for where there is no overt conflict there is usually little growth. However, a management philosophy of harmonious peace is, paradoxically, entirely appropriate for a growth company that is being run by a Maverick Executive. The company succeeds because the Maverick Executive, having surrounded himself with zombielike subordinates who are good technicians, makes all the decisions and sets the policies and everyone rides on his coattails. This type of centralized management is especially common in highly personalized businesses, such as cosmetics, fashion goods, and liquor.

However, the Maverick Executive, driving incessantly for his company's success in the market, does not realize that, internally, his company is anything but a peaceful and harmonious team. Although the over-dependent executives he has inevitably cultivated appear submissive to him, nearly all of them are in fierce conflict with each other and with their subordinates as well. The Maverick Executive remains unaware of these frictions and contests because he does not realize that with overdependent executives on his staff he cannot expect to know what is going on in any of the management levels below him. Those "ideal" supervisory types he prefers are, if anything, even poorer than he is at judging people. They manifest Mc-Murry's Law of Diminishing Competence: a weak superior invariably selects subordinates weaker than himself. In a tall organization this makes for extremely weak supervision at lower levels.

It is only very rarely that a Maverick Executive is able to recognize the nature and symptoms of his insecure subordinates. However, he may have to learn about them if his company is not doing well and if his directors carry enough weight to insist on an outsider's appraisal of its management. In that case, an objective appraisal could reveal a broad mixture and wide variety of overdependent executives. Each of them would exhibit one or two of a number of clearcut symptoms, but these five are nearly universal:

1. He becomes defensive in order to deny his insecurities.

2. He tends to be reactionary and overcautious and to cling to the past because he fears innovations.

3. He is indecisive because even the slightest risk arouses anxieties in him.

4. He is mindlessly conformist and bureaucratic because he needs the support of rules to bolster his indecisiveness.

5. As a leader, he is autocratic and authoritarian to conceal his inner uncertainties and to frighten his subordinates so they will submit to his demands and will not report on his shortcomings.

Perhaps even more easily spotted are two other telltale marks of the overdependent executive. One is his excessive preoccupation with his place on the organization chart and with the trappings that go with his job. The other is his inability to accept responsibility for anything that has gone wrong. With regard to the first, he becomes obsessed with the size and location of his office, its furnishings, and the various emoluments and privileges of his position. As for the second, he is invariably convinced that he is the victim of circumstances beyond his control; there must always be a scapegoat to take the blame, but he is never conscious of his contributing role in his difficulties.

The Maverick Executive who is advised of such behaviors is not likely to regard them seriously. He does not consider the personal weaknesses and feelings of his subordinates to be his responsibility, nor does he believe that he is a major contributor to their behaviors. And he is likely to be simply amused rather than concerned by the different species and subspecies of the overdependent executive to be found within his company. These include the Bureaucrats, among whom are the Old Faithfuls and the Decision-Escapers; the Clerks, who include the Sycophants and the Obsolete; and the Autocrats, who include the Two-faced and the Petty varieties. Each of these varieties is responsible for a different assortment of people problems, but the Maverick Executive usually knows nothing about such problems—unless one of them suddenly and directly interferes with his plans and directives. Then he has to cope with the hostilities and strategies of the overdependent executive.

He can expect to be opposed by one of two main strategies of the overdependent: a fight reaction or a flight from responsibility. The first takes one of two forms, either the tactic of passive aggression or that of passive resistance. An example of the passive aggression tactic occurred in one company whose new Maverick president was confident he could solve the company's loss of competitive position by developing a new product line and getting into a new field. He greatly respected his sales vice president and solicited his opinion because the company had very successfully used this executive's marketing tactics in the past. He did not know the man was an overdependent executive who felt immediately threatened by the president's plan, which would require him to operate in a field in which he did not feel competent. Typically, the vice president concealed his hostility and did not attack the plan openly. Instead, under the guise of "advising the president," he began planting questions in the president's mind. His most effective ploy was to point out that if the project failed, it might reflect on the president's good judgment. The tactic worked in this case, not because the president had any doubts about his project but because he incorrectly assessed the vice president's maneuver; he assumed the vice president was really voicing the objections of some key directors and, in typical Maverick fashion, he played his political hunch and killed his project.

Far more treacherous for the Maverick Executive is the strategy of passive resistance. This involves more devious measures by which the executive can attack his boss, and it is effective because he is very adept at concealing his motives. For example, in the situation described above, instead of using passive aggression the overdependent executive might have greeted the Maverick Executive's new project with great enthusiasm and launched it in an atmosphere of euphoria. Thereafter, however, nothing constructive would happen. The executive can see to it that interminable delays intervene, mistakes are made, misunderstandings occur. Each failure is then appropriately rationalized; whatever has happened, or failed to happen, is never the overdependent executive's fault but is the result of "circumstances beyond my control." He himself is usually not conscious of the extent of his hostility, but his prime objective is in fact to frustrate the Maverick Executive by rendering him ineffective in spite of his superior power and status.

Against this strategy of passive resistance, the Maverick Executive is often utterly powerless to take effective counteraction. Lacking perceptivity about people, he naively accepts at face value the feigned enthusiasm of an overdependent executive and his earnest apologies for the delays and foul-ups that can stall a project long enough to kill it. The Maverick Executive's drive to innovate and accomplish things

136

may be stopped cold when this same strategy is used in a labor dispute. The strategy was dramatically demonstrated in 1970 when the air controllers, in their campaign to force the government to improve their wages and working conditions, tied up all major airports by "working to rule."

The other main strategy of the overdependent executive, the flight from responsibility, can also be effective against a Maverick Executive. However, it rarely occurs because the Maverick Executive keeps decision making in his own hands, and if it does occur, it is usually easier even for him to detect. This maneuver, practiced daily in every government and nearly all business enterprises, includes a great many different tactics, but all of them are aimed to help the overdependent executive avoid decision making without loss of face. These tactics range from taking flight into detail, delegating problems to committees, or inducing the boss to commit himself on how to handle a problem to double talk, insisting on "getting all the facts," and taking to the bottle or to drugs.

While the Maverick Executive will neither see nor hear about most of the strategies and tactics of overdependent executives, these will certainly take their toll in productivity and damaged morale among their subordinates. Their pseudosupervision inevitably produces hostility and frustration, and employees who have lost their illusions about a boss's competence and fairness will usually turn to a union for protection. Moreover, sooner or later they discover that the Maverick Executive, despite his charismatic image and unusual capacities, is like any other chief executive whenever a dispute arises between an incompetent, overdependent executive and a subordinate: he will invariably support the person who is superior in rank —simply because he *is* superior in rank. The result of these frustrations may be chronic labor trouble.

This is the kind of trouble that, unfortunately, the Maverick Executive is least equipped to deal with. He naturally sees any union as an enemy that threatens to curb his authority, and he is very inclined to attack the enemy directly, ignoring the chain of conditions that lies behind almost every management-labor dispute. One very basic cause which he should attack, of course, is the proliferation of overdependent executives which his own behaviors and traits have consciously and unconsciously cultivated. He himself is, however, practically incapable of taking either of the two steps necessary to arrive at the proper therapy for his overdependent executives.

The first step—making an in-depth analysis of each overdependent executive personally—will be stoutly resisted by the Maverick Executive because he simply does not want to learn about the shortcomings of his subordinates who, after all, are normally his own appointees. A typical reaction expressed by one Maverick president to whom I had just handed a very unflattering assessment of a subordinate was: "I am very disappointed in your appraisal of Mr. X," implying directly that I, not the subordinate, was at fault. What he did not say was that the report did not tell him what he wished to hear, which was that the subordinate was fine and thus a credit to his boss's excellent judgment. This is what the usual chief executive expects to hear, and his resistance to negative assessments is a familiar self-defense technique that serves both to prevent others from learning of his limitations and to maintain his psychological equilibrium or homeostasis. The Maverick Executive, however, reacts to a critical assessment not in self-defense but in self-assurance; he does not "hear" it. He is always optimistic about his obedient subordinates and is sure they are doing their jobs well under his firm direction.

The Maverick Executive is also in all probability going to resist the second step needed to help his overdependent subordinates, which is a thorough assessment of their working conditions. However, since this is a more objective and less personal procedure, he may be persuaded by his directors to have such an analysis carried out. This involves the exploration and measurement of the six main parameters of each executive's position, namely: its technical requirements, special features (travel requirements, etc.), degree of structuring, opportunities for advancement, compensation, and its compatibility requirements. With all this information and a careful appraisal of the incumbent, a set of job specifications can be prepared that represent an ideal placement for the overdependent executive.

It can be safely assumed that few if any job openings in the company will exactly meet the executive's requirements, and also that a Maverick Executive will not countenance the creation of job openings in the hierarchy just to provide safe havens for his incompetent subordinates. (Yet there are companies that do so; a Midwestern railroad, for one, carried on the payroll 16 executive assistants to the president—

all failures as operating officers—for several years at a cost of $25,000 each.)

What a Maverick Executive is most likely to do, once he is shown the failings of an overdependent executive in his present position, is simply to shift him informally to some other, lesser job without any reasonably plausible rationalizations. This is almost certain to increase the man's anxiety, but he may be able to take it. In one case a 58-year-old executive who had been sales manager for 12 years was abruptly moved back to a staff job as training director. Although his salary was not cut, the shift constituted a considerable loss of face and was particularly abrasive to his ego. But with only seven years to go before retirement, and with practically no chance of getting an equally well-paying job elsewhere, rather than resign he swallowed his pride and took the staff job. A more humane technique is to shift the failing executive out of the company's mainstream and into an important sounding face-saving position. A chief engineer, for instance, might be made executive assistant to the vice president for engineering research.

To the practical mind of a Maverick Executive, however, such shifts are acceptable for only two reasons: they serve to salvage the executive's expertise and to keep him out of the hands of competitors. The Maverick Executive does not know that in his informal, often harsh ways he is practicing a crude version of what psychiatrists call "milieu therapy," which is to adapt the executive's job environment to meet the man's needs and values rather than the company's. Properly done, this therapy restructures and

clearly specifies the executive's new duties, responsibilities, reporting relationships, and authority, so
that he feels more congenial and secure. Usually, too,
the new job is arranged so that more or most of the
decisions are made by the executive's boss. Under a
Maverick Executive, however, this does not apply,
since all significant decision making is already in the
hands of the boss. Any executive he shifts, therefore,
becomes probably even more dependent on the Maverick Executive and gets his relief primarily from
having a smaller load of supervisory work.

There are several other measures for handling the
overdependent executive, but each faces hard going
under a Maverick Executive. One of these techniques
is to hire an ombudsman, preferably an outsider, perhaps a psychologist who is skillful in dealing with people. As a good listener the ombudsman can counsel
the insecure and mediate among feuding executives
and between executive levels. To a Maverick Executive, however, an ombudsman is likely to appear as
an interloper who comes between him and his subordinates and possibly undermines his authority over
them. Similarly, while the technique of making a
failing executive a consultant to the company may
retain his expertise and protect him from the competition, it cannot appeal to the Maverick Executive; he
is not given to taking the advice of outsiders and certainly won't listen attentively to an ex-subordinate who
has been removed from a job he couldn't handle.

On the other hand, a Maverick Executive has no
hesitation in applying the oldest technique of all for
handling a failing executive: separate him from the

company. Before doing so, however, the Maverick Executive has to be sure the man is really incompetent; he won't be disqualified just for exhibiting nervousness, indecision, or even gross inefficiency, but because he cannot perform reasonably well the specific tasks the Maverick Executive has assigned him. Other chief executives commonly procrastinate the firing of a veteran, obsolete executive who is liked by everyone in the company; he may be carried along for years and his final separation often causes intense guilt feelings among his colleagues. A Maverick Executive indulges in no such sentimental dawdling; he drops any executive as soon as he is convinced of his incompetence.

At the same time, a Maverick Executive—with a little outside assistance—can exhibit a large talent of his own for salvaging an insecure executive on his staff. While his drive and abounding self-confidence generally reassure his dependent, insecure subordinates, the bitter animosities among them often produce intense anxieties. Usually he remains quite unaware of these suffering subordinates, but if he hears about an individual case he can, with just a brief word of charismatic reassurance, sometimes accomplish astonishing results.

In one case a division president had reached a state of great anxiety (manifested by excessive drinking) while working under a corporate group vice president who disliked him and made no effort to conceal his hostility. The division president, who had been with the company for 25 years, had five children to put through school; he was under severe financial strain and was agonizing over the possibility of being fired. Fortunately—and most unusually—the board chairman, a Maverick, learned of the man's situation and called him in and warmly reassured him, saying that he regarded the man as very valuable and that there was no danger of his being dismissed. The effect was instantaneous. The man's behavior changed completely from despairing anxiety to beaming self-confidence.

This was one of the most incredible transformations ever observed personally by me, and it dramatically illustrates how, if a Maverick Executive is nudged, he can swiftly heal the very wounds of failing executives for which his insensitivity and management style are predominantly responsible. The trouble is that he, like most all other executives, has not yet learned that such salvage work is one of his basic obligations.

HOW HE GAINS
AND MAINTAINS POWER

8

The need for power is one of the inescapable facts of business life. Without power, an executive or manager has no authority; without authority, he is merely a figurehead and there can be no discipline; and without discipline, an organization becomes chaotic. I define power as the capacity to modify the conduct of employees in a desired manner, together with the capacity to avoid having one's own behavior modified in undesired ways by others. As James J. Cribbin puts it, the power an executive needs is "naught but the ability to impose one's will on others whether they like it or not." [1]

The Maverick Executive is acutely aware of the necessity for power. While every chief executive recognizes this need, the Maverick Executive's extraordinary drive to accomplish his goals in his own ways makes power absolutely essential for him. He expects

[1] *Effective Managerial Leadership* (New York: Amacom, 1972).

the cooperation of his subordinates, but if this is not forthcoming, he demands complete obedience. And even more essential for him is the influence he needs to gain over his superiors, particularly key directors and stockholders who might block his plans.

In addition, the Maverick Executive needs to resist pressures to change his own behavior. His great self-confidence is not enough, for he cannot depend on the goodwill of others, and some of his subordinates, while vying for his favor, may be privately planning to unseat him. As a hard realist he knows that duress will be required to secure their obedience and that it is sometimes necessary to treat even key employees as serfs—they may be transferred at his will, assigned to a nomadic existence on the road for months at a time, and even required to adopt a standard of living determined basically by him. Even their jobs are expendable at his direction. However, he also knows that subordinates can counteract his orders with passive resistance and other strategies. Once he gains the top position, a Maverick Executive becomes the major target of stratagems by subordinates and others both within and outside the company. His capacity for recognizing and coping with such threats is one of the marks of his stature as a Maverick Executive.

Like any other chief executive who has little or no equity in the business he is managing, the Maverick Executive has very little security. He will be the scapegoat if the business falters or fails. The hard fact is that the only hope for survival for one in the top position is to become expert in strategies and tactics that are basically political and often Machiavellian.

Generally speaking, the concept of the need for power over others is not highly regarded in the American culture. People who are concerned with the acquisition, use, and maintenance of power are often regarded with suspicion; their objectives are somehow considered to be "not nice" or a bit antisocial or worse. To some, the gaining, retaining, and wielding of power over others smack of ruthlessness and deception. Nevertheless, such acts are required of anyone who intends to become and remain a chief executive. Enthusiasm for democratizing business management has often minimized or entirely obliterated the fact, but that attitude toward the role of power is highly unrealistic.

Ambitious executives are versed in a score or more of strategies and tactics for securing and retaining power, and the Maverick Executive is an expert at many of them. However, some of them he characteristically employs quite differently. Others he does not use at all, and he is notably weak in several of the ways and means of enforcing his dictates and protecting his job. Some of the techniques described here are simple, others relatively complex, but all of them I have observed in use by executives managing a wide variety of businesses, and they have proved effective more often than not in the tough world of competitive enterprise.

1. *He adamantly insists on an employment contract.* Whether he is being promoted to the top job from within the company or is brought in from the outside, the Maverick Executive demands such an agreement, not only to establish his job security and his authority,

but because it shows his employers he is not submissive and will not be overridden. Many companies today prefer to sign on a new chief executive with only a gentlemanly handshake as the binder, and CBS's young Maverick President Taylor agreed to this, but a more experienced Maverick Executive does not run the risks involved, especially since he is often asked to rehabilitate or salvage a failing operation or initiate one in an entirely new field where failure is very likely. If the project turns sour, the Maverick Executive—whether he is to blame or not—is a natural scapegoat, likely to be sacked without hesitation unless he has an employment contract.

2. *He does* not *obtain from his employers a concise, specific job description.* Other chief executives normally ask for a clear, unambiguous written statement of the duties, responsibilities, authority, and reporting relationships of the new assignment. However, the Maverick Executive wants no such straitjacket; he wants to be entirely free to make the job develop according to his own specifications and to be able to expand it in any direction he desires. He wants nothing less than a statement giving him full authority as commander in chief, and counts on his charisma and maneuvering skills to overcome or bypass any informal restrictions that the directors or senior officers may try to impose on him.

3. *He makes sure he is compatible with his superiors.* On his way to the top position a Maverick Executive takes pains to discover the values, goals, and personal likes and dislikes of those in a position to help him advance. Often he attracts the backing of an im-

portant sponsor who can build up his image in the top echelons. Unlike other ambitious executives, he does not try to conform as closely as possible to what his superiors are looking for; he will not attempt to hide his dynamic self-reliance from a superior who expects him to be passively submissive. But he is careful, too. If he knows that a particular boss can sabotage his future, he will observe the rule that is inviolate for other executives: never tell your boss anything he does not wish to hear or believe until you are sure he can tolerate it.

If the Maverick Executive is being recruited to fill a top spot, he will, before he joins the company, see that he becomes acquainted with his future superiors —directors and major stockholders—informally on the golf course, tennis courts, or during business conferences he may be asked to attend. He checks whether their prejudices and expectations are congenial or abrasive to him, and at the first sign of significant incompatibility he will call off the negotiations. He knows that incompatibility almost inevitably grows worse in time.

Unlike most prospective chief executives, the Maverick Executive does not worry if his wife happens to dislike—or displease—the wives of important directors or officers. His insensitivity to people makes him regard such frictions as unimportant and he believes (sometimes incorrectly) that nothing of this sort could be detrimental to the appraisal of his own qualifications.

4. *He establishes strong alliances with influential outsiders.* The Maverick Executive, like other chief

executives, seeks to develop strong relationships not only with influential directors and stockholders but with key executives in banks, insurance companies, or others who may have power to affect company policies and finances. He may, as one Maverick does, court the steady approval of the founder's widow by having lunch with her once a month, or he may take up some hobby that interests a key director. He may also cultivate acquaintances among senators, congressmen, and heads of government departments or trade associations who could affect his plans.

However, unlike other ambitious executives, he does not develop close alliances with any of his peers or subordinates in the company. He is basically a loner and does not really trust any of his associates in the business except one or two protégés he has carefully tested for their submissiveness and unwavering, dependent loyalty. Such passive dependents are further bound to him by having their job responsibilities defined in such a way that their future security depends completely on their cooperation and obedience.

5. *He takes great care to find reliable, technically expert subordinates who regard him as a father figure.* The preference of the Maverick Executive for submissive subordinates has already been noted. Their loyalty to him is based on the recognition that their job security and financial future depend on the Maverick's retaining his power. They do not love him, they may even be intensely ambivalent toward him, but they need him. Since it takes some time to build a cadre of such subordinates, the Maverick Execu-

tive often brings several close associates with him when he moves to another company.

He is also careful to avoid having a strong No. 2 man on his staff. His own decisiveness and abrasiveness naturally assure this, because they tend to drive off people who are in conflict with him. Other chief executives now tend to accept the theory that they should develop a strong, competent No. 2 man to take over if they should leave the company or be unable to function temporarily. But the Maverick does not risk or invite any challenge to his authority.

6. *He controls his subordinates with the power of the purse.* The Maverick Executive, like most chief executives who retain their power, keeps a close fiscal grip on the activities of his subordinates. By disapproving a departmental budget, he can bring any project and its promoter quickly into line, and by approving a budget, he can further increase a subordinate's dependency and grateful support. One technique cited by Antony Jay that is used by executives who have recently taken over a corporation is to give money-hungry subordinates more money for their projects but to attach certain conditions, such as requiring them to supply him with more information or to refer more decisions to him.[2] The Maverick Executive, unlike most executives, does not shrink from simple bribery of this kind.

7. *He does not encourage the development of open channels of downward communication.* The Maverick Executive is closemouthed. He has learned the dangers

[2] *Management and Machiavelli,* p. 48.

of communication, that many things should not be revealed. He takes great care to limit the passing of information to those whose use of it will not be disadvantageous to him. His political sense warns him against revealing bad news that may cause his subordinates to lose confidence in his leadership. He recognizes that there are no secrets in an organization for long. Anything "revealed in confidence" will probably be known to nearly everyone in the company—and many outside—by the next day. He knows that a subordinate who is privy to confidential information is potentially the most dangerous threat of all, since his release of this material, either by design or by accident, can be disastrous.

Conversely, his efforts to communicate are often very clumsy and upsetting. He may announce an important shift in his staff assignments without foreseeing the painful effect this will have on subordinates whose status has been suddenly altered. In fact, the Maverick Executive is extremely weak and vulnerable in the entire area of getting and giving information, and in this respect he differs from most ambitious executives. Yet his secrecy and reticence certainly give him great power.

8. *He gets and goes his own way at all times.* The tremendous drive of the Maverick Executive is to accomplish his own objectives and to do this to perfection, as he sees it. His single-mindedness shows up in distinct ways that often violate the precepts of orthodox executive behavior.

—He is very cautious about taking advice from others, knowing that advice can be disguised pressure, aimed to influence him to delegate decisions to others. He considers the advice of specialists potentially useful, never decisive, since it can easily lead to their usurping enough of his power to make them dangerous to his command.

—He is not open-minded to contrary opinions. He does not welcome such views, even though they may be the means by which he might correct a course that is leading to disaster. He is not concerned about giving the impression of being fair, especially to his opponents. He will not listen patiently while a subordinate is talking on a subject he knows about; instead, he may aggressively question the subordinate to prove the rightness of his own ideas.

—He does not compromise on small matters or make temporary concessions for the sake of future advances. He is stubborn about the smallest details, knowing that these can readily jeopardize his plans. Though such stubbornness can be disastrous, the Maverick Executive takes the risk in his drive for perfection.

—He can be quite flexible in interpreting company rules, which he considers of no decisive importance. He knows that if he is to win and hold the allegiance of his subordinates, he must be willing to bend the rules occasionally at least, making exceptions when he feels they are justified.

—He can be ruthless when it is expedient. He is never a "nice guy" to his subordinates, who know that he can be tough and exacting in his demands. By fairly and firmly administering discipline, he wins from his subordinates the respect and trust he must have to gain their obedient cooperation. He will take prompt and decisive action in a crisis; he feels no remorse in closing down a plant that is losing money, even though the local community may be heavily dependent on its payroll.

—He never commits himself completely or irrevocably. He is very expert in adapting to changed conditions and circumstances. His flexibility accounts for much of his success as an operating, enterprising chief. He knows that even his major alliances are not fixed and is prepared to lose some sponsors and gain new ones when the situation demands it. Unlike many executives, he does not permit friendships to tie him to a course or project that becomes unprofitable. He is especially wary of establishing too close bonds with protégés.

9. *He influences, manipulates, and uses subordinates and others to maintain power to gain his ends.* The Maverick Executive's attitudes toward other people are primarily determined by their power to hurt or help him. He may be paternalistic, imperious, political, ingratiating, or impersonal, depending on his assessment of the relationship.

—He avoids fraternization of any kind with subordinates and has no very close personal relations with others in his business life. He thinks he is objective in matters concerning his docile subordinates, but he is actually mistrustful of even his protégés. The door to his office may be "open" but no one in the company would dare to enter it without his permission. He may attend social occasions and appear informal and relaxed but he never forgets the protocol of his position; usually he remains tense and more absorbed in his own thoughts than in what he may be talking about at the time.

—He uses the ploy of passive resistance to block pressures on him from his directors or influential stockholders. If pressed to take action on something he regards as inadvisable, he may sidestep an open confrontation by stalling. He may initiate action but by his tactics he will insure that what he opposes will suffer endless delays and ultimately die.

—He never fully trusts the loyalty of his subordinates, except those who are his protégés. He does not count on a subordinate's loyalty unless he knows it represents a personal advantage to the subordinate. He has found that most people are not compulsively conscientious; they may pay lip service to him, but their real loyalty is always to themselves and their interests. When the stakes are high, he trusts no one but himself.

His wariness makes him alert to threats to his authority that can come from those who are aggressively ambitious, who have antipathies toward authority, who are malcontents and, most especially, those whom he has been forced to discipline or demote. Such subordinates, aware of his arbitrariness, usually conceal their tactics and often mislead him with incomplete or faulty information. As one retiring Maverick said to his successor, "Yesterday was the last time you heard the truth."

—He protects his power by eliminating all potential rivals. On taking over as chief executive, his first step may be to remove as promptly as possible every subordinate who is even remotely identified with the previous boss or his close associates. Though they may be experienced and competent, their values will probably conflict with the Maverick's and their loyalty to him will remain suspect. He has learned the hard truth that nothing is more threatening to power than chronic sabotage in the ranks and the slow, poisonous influence of the disloyal.

—He does not believe in giving praise as well as censure. Unlike many chief executives, he does not try to temper the sting of criticism with encouraging comments about a man's usual good job. He expects his subordinates to turn in first-rate performances all the time and is concerned only with their lapses. He believes that praising a subordinate tends to induce complacency and to diminish the anxiety tensions to achieve what the Maverick wants—top performance continuously.

10. *He dramatizes and sells himself to others.* The Maverick Executive is very aware of the necessity to impress not only his subordinates but all those who can further his career and simultaneously help the company prosper. While his drive and self-confidence naturally produce an image that asserts his power, he skillfully employs his other attributes to enhance that image.

—He is an adept actor who is aware of his charisma and its influence on others. He always gives the impression that he knows what he is doing and is in complete command of the situation, even though he may not be all that sure. He knows that his subordinates look to him to protect the security of their jobs and that he dares not give any indication of being indecisive if he wants to not only maintain but enhance his power. He perpetually radiates self-confidence.

—He has honed his skill as a salesman to razor sharpness. In conversing with important persons and in speaking to groups, he has learned to apply a prime lesson of salesmanship by finding out what his listeners want and value and what they are interested in. However, he also intuitively senses people's fears and prejudices and quite openly plays on them.

—He exhibits the signs of his status, power, and success. He knows that he cannot be too modest or democratic in his life-style because this may be mistaken for a lack of power and influence. But unlike the overstriving executive, he is comparatively modest. He may spend heavily on a hobby like sports-car racing, sailing, or horse breeding, but he does not build a big mansion or drive a Rolls Royce to impress his subordinates and others. Nor does he need such conspicuous consumption to reassure himself. He may drive himself to work in a Cadillac or any car that is available; one Maverick used his daughter's Volkswagen while his car was laid up for repairs.

To a great many people in management, including chief executives, many of these strategies and tactics of political maneuvering may seem distasteful, or undemocratic, or hypocritical. But the use of power in handling others is a reality; every management must have it in some degree and use it. The Maverick Executive uses many of these techniques more blatantly than other chief executives, for he is convinced, as all great leaders have been, that without a high

159

degree of centralized, essentially autocratic power, no enterprise can function effectively. His alertness and skill in using these strategies do not, in themselves, make him successful; some of them may even blunt his effectiveness. But without them he would be severely, perhaps irretrievably, handicapped by his inherent deficiencies, most especially by his insensitivity to people and his inability to judge and communicate with others.

Moreover, the Maverick Executive is an unrelenting realist. He accepts the world as it is and does not attempt to work with rosy, unrealistic assumptions about human beings in organizations. He bases his exercise of power on the ancient and still prevailing fact that power is inevitably linked with fear. If people weren't afraid of having their circumstances modified in an extremely disagreeable way, most of them would not obey commands. Obedience is a dirty word among young members of modern society, who think of it as simply bowing to another's orders. They do not recognize its necessity in every organized activity. Without it, the power of any leader is instantly disrupted, and without strong leadership, there is chaos, decay, and failure.

The Maverick Executive is, above all, a strong leader. And since he is ill equipped to win the voluntary, democratic cooperation of all his subordinates (some can never identify with him and be susceptible to leadership by influence), he strives to gain and maintain the power that secures obedience. Paradoxically, the more skillful he is in applying his power-winning strategies and tactics, the more cooperative most of his subordinates will become; they trade their submissiveness for the security he offers them. Indeed, he may maneuver so adroitly that many people do not even think of obedience to him but only of helping to make the organization function well in order to accomplish what the Maverick Executive has planned. These are, in his view, the ideal subordinates who prove the virtues of his power.

HIS BASIC
INTOLERANCE

9

The most serious problem facing the Maverick Executive has its roots in his greatest weakness: his intolerance of other people's values. Neither his blindness in communications nor his poor judgment of personnel nor his inability to delegate is as ominous for him as his almost total inability to understand and deal with the conflicts between his own rigidly held values and those held by others. In heightened degree, his values are the ones subscribed to by most senior executives, so that the Maverick Executive's blindness in this respect can be seen as a caricature of a generic affliction of executives, one for which no one yet has found any reasonable cure.

The problem is simply stated, but there is nothing simple about its causes. The Maverick Executive is an unbending advocate of the work ethic and cannot accept the fact that many employees subscribe to a value system that is the polar opposite of his own. He believes absolutely that "decent" people have a respect for authority, work hard, and are diligent in carrying out their responsibilities. They are persons of integrity who lead moral lives; they are frugal and live within their incomes; they take pride in their work; and they conform reasonably to the mores of the prevailing culture. These are the beliefs the Maverick Executive expects his subordinates to hold, and indeed those who do are the kind of obedient, conscientious, loyal, and productive workers that every executive is looking for.

The trouble is that in the last twenty years these shibboleths of the work ethic have suffered such erosion that job performance and moral standards have deteriorated at all levels. Long before the startling exposures of the Watergate fiasco in 1972, management ethics were crumbling, with executives, for example, no longer hesitating to steal ideas, data, or accounts from their employers. But the shift in values has been even more serious among members of the younger generation, many of whom have manifested nihilism, crusadism, and hedonism. Respect for discipline, conformity, order, and consideration for others has been replaced in many cases by a search for "self-realization" whose goal, more often than not, is "happiness," which often enough is a euphemism for unadulterated pleasure-seeking. In my forty years of interviewing candidates for all types of positions, I have observed a radical shift of attitudes toward work and responsibility. In the thirties, a job seeker was prepared to do anything an employer might require. In the seventies, the question is no longer, "What must I do to keep my job?" but "How is the company going to satisfy *my* needs and wants?"

Because of such shifts in values, top executives everywhere have been faced with a critical challenge to their authority. For those concerned with management development the challenge is critical precisely because these new values are encountered most often among the more alert, technically competent, and analytically minded young persons who have been recruited as candidates for ultimate advancement into top management positions. In the 1970s, many management trainees have goals and expectations that are radically different from those of their parents. They seek a high degree of autonomy, exhibit less loyalty and dedication to their employer, and want not only to participate in the leadership of the enterprise but also to share in the equity their efforts have helped to produce and win immediate rewards.

To the Maverick Executive these ideas and attitudes are presumptuous and naive. Like other self-made men, he is convinced that hard work and taking orders from others are essentials for any aspiring manager, but in addition, his compulsive, energetic temperament and drive for accomplishment make him far more devoted to the work ethic than other executives. He is not, as already pointed out, concerned with developing competent, independent managers; he believes managers will learn for themselves under his leadership. He would quite agree that perhaps nearly a quarter of all the bright, sophisticated college graduates are either totally unemployable in business because of their extremist, antibusiness, alienated, or hedonistic attitudes, or they are marginal prospects who would experience difficulty in adapting themselves permanently to the discipline and demands of business. The Maverick Executive would also agree that such persons, despite their superior endowments, do not belong in business in any case.

Nevertheless, he still has to cope with the attitudes of all those subordinates who, in some degree at least, now question the authority of management and tend to disparage the standards by which the Maverick Executive grew up. As one young M.B.A. said, "The Puritan ethic was a facade, an excuse for greed and self-righteousness. It is a front for the fact that most people don't have the imagination and/or creativity to devise their own life-style." To the Maverick Executive such talk is gibberish; a life-style that was good enough for the leaders he so admires is more than good enough for him, and he is highly suspicious of those who talk about imagination and creativity, for these are terms he associates with artists, writers, and others he regards as impractical, lazy, and undisciplined. His stereotyped thinking about people is, however, perhaps the least serious obstacle he faces in trying to deal with the new attitudes of his subordinates.

Indeed, the Maverick Executive is at an incredible disadvantage whenever he attempts to meet the problem of making employee values conform with his. Like other chief executives he has to face the fact that management no longer has leverage over the subordinate provided by traditional economic pressures. In this era of affluence, employees no longer submit to management's orders for fear of losing their jobs. Jobs are still not too difficult for educated, upper-middle-class people to secure. And to a greater or lesser degree, thousands more subsist on public welfare.

Furthermore, the Maverick Executive cannot now rely on measures that once stimulated employees to work better. Appeals to pride in workmanship, respect for quality, loyalty to company tradition, and so forth, are largely empty phrases to subordinates who may change jobs several times before they find a work environment that they feel is compatible. Many have been preconditioned by uninformed teachers and professors who advance such charges against management as this, reported by a young job seeker: "Marketing is the parasite fringe of the economy because it adds nothing to the value of the product, and is antisocial because it induces people to buy things they do not want, do not need, and cannot afford."

Yet these are by no means the most formidable obstacles a Maverick Executive faces in this conflict of values. There are many more serious difficulties, and all are traceable to weaknesses in himself.

He is unaware of the basic psychological facts about values. He does not know that many values are purely fictional, such as "all men are created equal"; that many of his values are contradictory; that he is in large measure the prisoner of his own values; that people do not tolerate other people's values; that opposing values can be substituted when conditions change; that values are inhibiting, that they can compel obedience and instill guilt feelings; that values are impervious to logic or reason. By his behavior, attitudes, and opinions the Maverick Executive explicitly demonstrates the validity of these facts about values.

1. He subscribes to values and ideas that have no counterpart in reality. He believes, for instance, that "The end justifies the means." Thus he may fire a veteran subordinate who is costing the company money because he cannot do his job as quickly or as well as he once did. Or he will oppose laws to protect the environment from pollution if such laws promise to lessen the company's ability to maintain its former profit margin.

2. The values he adheres to while in the office may flatly contradict those he expresses while in social or holiday situations. At a morning meeting in his office he may solemnly affirm highly moralistic sentiments concerning gentlemanly conduct with ladies; then at lunch after several martinis he may proudly recount his own experiences with women. And in the evening, after flying to a convention in Las Vegas, he may become involved in some crude sexual exploits.

3. He unwittingly and automatically makes serious decisions based on emotional judgments. He may decide to acquire a small company in a moribund industry, telling his staff that this will challenge their ingenuity, while refusing to admit to himself that he wants to acquire this company because as a boy he always admired their products.

4. He is very intolerant toward values that contradict his own. His mind is closed on certain subjects about which he can be extremely obstinate. Even in the face of absolute proof he may continue to disagree "as a matter of principle." Ideas that deviate even slightly from those he acquired in his association with peers and from emulated "heroes" he considers un-

acceptable, and a deviation such as smoking pot or promiscuous sexual adventures shocks him.

5. He shifts his values to suit the circumstances. On Sunday morning in church he is imbued with ideas of honest conduct and deplores those who rob and cheat. But on weekdays he can readily rationalize business practices that may delude and exploit the company's customers and reduce the value of its products.

6. He acquires values from stories about heroes he admires and feels guilty if he fails to live up to those ideals. His respect for heroic, pioneering achievement often leads him to attempt what cannot be done without enormous sacrifice by others as well as by himself. If the project fails, the guilt he feels is directed against his personal shortcomings, not the frustrations and losses endured by his subordinates and others associated with him.

7. His values are rarely produced by or changed by logic or reason. His superconfidence sometimes gives him a compulsion to convert others—or force them to submit—to his points of view. He is very hostile to youthful attitudes toward work, responsibility, and private property; he thinks nonconforming, antiauthoritarian young people are not amenable to logic and the facts as he sees them, and that therefore the only alternative is to use force against them. He is certain that he himself is logical and responds to reason; yet he can simultaneously believe that young men with beards and long hair are anathema and that the portrait of the company's bushy-bearded founder hanging in his office is a reassuring symbol of honest tradition.

The Maverick Executive's values are directly reflected in his wishful thinking and erroneous beliefs about subordinates. These concepts are often naively illogical. He may, for instance, believe that telling employees how much the company has spent on new equipment, pensions, health and hospital insurance, and other fringe benefits will actually make them grateful and cooperative. Or he may believe that most of his subordinates are fond of him. If an employee opinion poll shows him that their real attitudes and feelings are different from what he expected, that they are critical of him and the company, he finds this incomprehensible and may even dispute the findings.

Some of his other beliefs involve ideas that are not only obsolete, they were never valid. His disinterest in management training and executive development is traceable in large measure to his conviction that everyone really desires to better himself and everyone can do so—as he believes *he* has done—if he only puts his mind to it. To the Maverick Executive, the command of the Delphic oracle "Know thyself" means simply that everyone should work hard and strive onward and upward. He himself is a prime exhibit of what might be called the Excelsior syndrome.

His ideas about motivating subordinates are also oversimplified fallacies: he believes that the most effective ways to influence people are to appeal to their better natures or to their greed for money. In his opinion, everyone has the same values and goals, so that whatever has inspired him to succeed (usually money) should also be effective in stimulating others to comparable efforts. Since he does not recognize the diverse complications of individual motives, he uses the same logic and appeals for everyone when presenting a new plan or project, and he expects each to respond with equal enthusiasm—which they all rather quickly learn to do.

The Maverick Executive's opinions about the value of education are not shared by many other executives. Unlike them, he does not believe that a college education invariably insures superior competence on the job. Nor does he equate intelligence with judgment and assume that because someone has a high IQ and is well trained, the soundness of his judgment is correspondingly enhanced. He is inherently inclined to distrust M.B.A.'s; he considers them too inexperienced, too intellectual, and often too arrogant, and he senses that they lack the hard-nosed practical judgment he has developed. Besides, he is aware that most of them are in a great hurry to become top executives and run their own shows, and he does not want hyper-aggressive men like that on his team.

Perhaps the most obvious of the Maverick Executive's beliefs about subordinates is his conviction that they should be handled forcefully and unequivocally. He believes that the submission and conformity of employees must be maintained and in his view the best means of insuring this is by direct and forceful confrontation, reinforced by threats of punishment. He thinks this is also the best way to change their beliefs and attitudes to conform with his own. In any argument he may have with subordinates, the final decision must be a zero-sum victory for him and his management; otherwise it constitutes an intolerable loss of face. In short, he insists on the kind of autocratic rule that is basic to his leadership.

In this respect he resembles a great many chief executives who regularly ignore those basic facts about the giving and taking of orders which the late Chester I. Barnard so cogently pointed out.[1] According to Barnard, if an order is to be carried out it is imperative that it meet four conditions: it must be understood, it must be consistent with the values of the one who is to carry it out, it must be perceived as being to his advantage, and it must be within his power to carry out.

Autocratic order giving is now obsolete as far as many young managers are concerned. They believe that authority is acquired not simply by rank or seniority but by experience and knowledge of the work to be done, and by concern for the welfare of subordinates and society. Paradoxically, the Maverick Executive personally appears to meet most of their criteria: he has much experience and knowledge of the work, and in a paternalistic way he has concern for subordinates taken as a whole. He is short on concern for society, but the quality he most definitely lacks is what young managers now want the most: the willingness to delegate the authority for risk taking and decision making. With little experience, some knowledge, and an idealized concern for world benefits, the ambitious young manager wants to participate in run-

[1] *The Functions of the Executive* (Cambridge: Harvard University Press, 1938).

174

ning the business. To the Maverick Executive, this is childish presumption.

Moreover, he does not recognize any need to loosen his grip on the managerial bridle. He does not see the implications in the conflicts between his values and the values of those who soft-pedal the Theory X type of authoritarian management and encourage the Theory Y type of participative management. To be sure, the shift toward participative management is still more in the realm of verbal acknowledgment than in actual practice. Currently the policy appears to be losing popularity, and the entire concept of hierarchical management—a concept which has characterized industry since the onset of the industrial revolution and which the Maverick Executive lives by—may be coming back into vogue. Changes that can now be seen—intensive selection and assessment techniques, job enrichment, sensitivity training, and so forth—are largely tangential. Subsequent changes in the attitudes and thinking of managers and employees are difficult to predict. However, it is notable that while the Maverick Executive is intolerant of these new ideas about management, he holds fast to one concept that seems likely to endure: every organization requires structured jobs, disciplined employees, and direction, essentially authoritarian, by the most competent and decisive authority available.

The Maverick Executive is so fully confident that he is the one to lead his organization that he remains intolerant of interference. His values are so deeply rooted in him that any effort to change them involves changing his whole personality, his goals and relationships with people. He recognizes this instinctively and is very resistant to any psychological analyses of the problems of his management. However, he is not like the overstriving executive who rejects such approaches because they make him anxious and doubtful about his own capacities; the Maverick Executive rejects them because he does not understand them, regards them as impractical, and senses they could interfere with the way he intends to manage everything.

To most executives, the Maverick Executive's values and attitudes sound very old fashioned, and in some large corporations his autocratic views and methods would not be tolerated, now or in the future. And he himself cannot be expected to change; indeed, he remains quite incapable of taking the steps essential to dealing with conflicts in values. He cannot be tolerant and objective about issues, he cannot calmly assess either his own or his antagonists' positions, and he will not diplomatically compromise his values in order to arrive at a mutually acceptable solution. His intransigence, in short, is practically total. He is both an anachronism and a paradox. Theoretically he should fail, but he does not. Indeed, the astonishing fact remains: in spite of himself he makes an extraordinarily successful chief executive because he knows and uses, often quite unintentionally, some very old-fashioned but basically sound techniques of management and leadership.

THE SECRETS
OF HIS LEADERSHIP

10

The Maverick Executive's style of leadership is actually a distinctive mixture of three different styles. He has some of the characteristics of the old-fashioned, high-handed autocratic father figure, some characteristics of the driving entrepreneur, and some characteristics of the inspirational hero. His leadership is often very difficult to take, not only for his subordinates but for his superiors, and his leadership qualities may easily escape a chief executive who must endure the abrasiveness and nonconformity of a Maverick on his staff. As Antony Jay puts it:

> It does take considerable wisdom on the part of [his] senior executive to realize that because this man is difficult to work over, he is not necessarily difficult to work under, and that the unlovable qualities may yet be of greater value to the corporation than the smooth charm of his complacent contemporaries; and that arrogance, stubbornness, and in-

subordination are only self-confidence, determination, and initiative with a coating of disapproval.[1]

Long before he becomes a chief executive, a Maverick Executive has learned some essential lessons about
leadership. He naturally tends to begin as an autocrat,
and he is often a self-appointed leader in his own
groups. He learns that with autocratic leadership he
can maintain control and induce that mixed sense of
fear, respect, and dependence in his subordinates that
will compel them to follow his directions in spite of
themselves. And he finds it very difficult to change
this manner of command; he is usually pretty well
locked in by his personality and his goals.

Like the entrepreneur, the Maverick Executive
forms his own style of personal leadership and acquires his particular value system through identification with the men and heroes he admires. That system
makes certain goals imperative, especially those of
money, status, and power. He learns that the most
effective way to accomplish something is to drive
himself hard and do the thing himself. Like the entrepreneur, he is aggressive and sublimates his aggressions
by working very hard. And he does this because, like
the entrepreneur, he has found that the technique
works and he can get jobs done this way.

But the Maverick Executive has developed an even
more powerful style of leadership—and has learned his
greatest secret—by becoming an inspiring, heroic type

[1] *Management and Machiavelli*, p. 164.

of leader. As such he exerts leadership by *influence*, the kind that an inspiring leader employs so that in spite of his limitations, he attracts and holds followers through the power of his charisma and the impressiveness of his positive qualities. Such leadership is not so much by design as it is a by-product of the leader's superior qualifications.

It is this leadership style by influence that most distinguishes the Maverick Executive from the old-time autocrats, the overstrivers, and the overaggressive entrepreneurs. More flexible than these types, he can occasionally shift his manner and approach, whereas nearly all those aggressive, inner-directed leaders who have built businesses have been confirmed, and not always benevolent, autocrats, inflexible in their style of leadership. And while a Maverick Executive drives himself and others for pragmatic reasons, he is not, like the overstriving executive, motivated by hate—or aggression, to use the more elegant psychological term. The overstriver, for example, may have been scorned or neglected as the young son of poor immigrant parents, and the bitterness remains. "You don't know what it is," one executive said, "to grow up poor and be called 'that Greek kid.'" But in a Maverick Executive, it is his tremendous inherent optimism, ambition, and courage that so strikingly produce strong, inner-directed action. At the same time, his self-confidence is infectious. His subordinates gain self-assurance merely by being associated with him.

The Maverick Executive has by no means achieved ideal leadership. This would be leadership by consciously and fully developed influence. Any executive who could achieve this would have to be a complete master of management. The Maverick Executive definitely is not that. He is in large measure a leader without knowing why; he thinks he knows, but many of his convictions are obviously wrong, particularly those that are founded on clichés and false beliefs about people.

Moreover, the Maverick Executive has only partially mastered the essential for leadership by means of management adaptability. He is skilled in only one style of management—benevolent autocracy—and so is not able to apply appropriate management styles to different kinds of employees. He is, in fact, not perceptive and sensitive enough to recognize and exploit constructively the psychological makeup and the diverse needs and values of those he is expected to lead. These psychological groups differ widely in their values, dependency, and acceptance or rejection of authority, and they range from the passive employee to the militant activist. Here are the groups and their characteristics in brief:

The passive employee is the docile, obedient worker for whom job security is paramount.

The hyperconscientious, compulsive perfectionist has very rigid values that often compel him to punish himself when he violates them. He has a powerful, punitive superego and is a superlative worker.

The moderately conscientious worker has a system of values that make him a good citizen, but he has no values that drive him compulsively to work and conform.

The mild hedonist usually is young and has a vague

182

goal of seeking "happiness" as the ultimate objective. His values tend to rationalize his self-indulgence. *The free spirit* is hostile to supervisory restrictions and not amenable to discipline. Supervision "bugs" him.

The militant activist has a free-floating, diffuse, but often powerful hostility that can be focused on many things fortuitously—parents, school, society, the boss, and so on. He hates the Establishment and is strongly opposed to discipline of any sort. He may even be overtly destructive and is sometimes active in labor or other protest groups.

Ideally, a chief executive recognizes that he cannot manage these different types of employees with a uniform style of leadership. The astute manager uses, for example, fairly autocratic leadership for passive employees to stir them to activity, but for the hyperconscientious types he uses a laissez faire form of leadership and counts on their perfectionism, self-motivation, and skills to hold them in line with the organization's procedures and goals. The Maverick Executive, however, treats all six of these distinct personality types in his benevolently autocratic style. But he sees to it that his subordinate managers know that he expects them to weed out the free spirits and the militant activists.

Actually, the Maverick Executive recognizes only two kinds of employees. One kind comprises key managers who know the business, are dependable, intelligent, and reasonably decisive, and with whom he can discuss his plans on occasion. These employees are a very small part of that limited number (probably not more than 10 or 20 percent of those who work for wages) who are basically self-reliant and seek challenges and responsibilities. Under most chief executives, such employees want to be on a team with a boss whom they must also admire, respect, and trust. They like to believe they are coordinate with, rather than subordinate to, him. Under a Maverick Executive, however, some of these employees may learn to curb their desire for autonomy and participation and accept his paternalistic direction, either as protégés or as highly paid specialists.

The other kind of employee identified by the Maverick Executive comprises that vast majority who are to some degree passive and dependent, insecure economically, needful of structure and support, and prone to feelings of worthlessness which they must simultaneously satisfy and deny. Many of these people are ambivalent both to him and to the enterprise; they have very conventional standards and a great scorn for values and standards that differ from their own. They are simultaneously both hostile and submissive toward authority and oppose whatever is soft and considerate of others; they maintain a selfish calculating and bargaining orientation toward others; they are intellectually rigid and they cannot tolerate ambiguity, since it creates anxiety in them.

The Maverick, to be sure, does not see this kind of employee so analytically. He is not aware that the typical employee wants not only material security and support but also recognition and prestige to bolster his ego; that he wants the leader to evidence supportive concern for him personally, and also needs the backing of this group. But the Maverick Executive is aware that most employees want to get ahead with a minimum of personal effort and that they prefer regimentation on the job because it relieves them of responsibility. The Maverick is less aware that the typical employee also seeks a strong and ruthless leader both to provide the security he needs and to gratify his needs for submission. But the Maverick is clearly aware that such employees need someone they can look up to, admire, and emulate, and whom in consequence they will obey, often to the point of sacrificing their self-interests. He does not know that they have a deep emotional need to obey and to admire a strong leader, or that they cannot tolerate weak leadership because it frightens them, or that they will not even acknowledge his weaknesses so long as these are not too obvious. If he is their hero and model, they will see him as strong even though he manifestly is not. The Maverick Executive intuitively senses what most employees want in a leader and he provides it in his fashion, which is predominantly that of an idealized father figure.

However, although he is not conscious of his resemblance to the image of the righteous and terrible ruler, a modern-day Yahweh, he often exhibits his traits as well as those of the legendary entrepreneurs who built and ruled their companies with an iron hand. Typical of them was the man who founded his company in 1922 and remained its chief executive until 1971. He was known as Moses to his staff and to his four sons, and his Mosaic rule was obvious: he set the company's goals, established the structures in which it operated, enforced his dictates absolutely, and was incapable of delegating any authority, although he did assign responsibility. Yet he was admired and widely emulated.

Although the Maverick Executive has many more capacities and qualities than the absolute autocrat, it is notable that even such a chief executive can nevertheless inspire many followers to admire him. For people tend to read or project into his actions those qualities and traits they are looking for. They feel the need to endow him with the capacities they want to see in their leader. In view of this psychological fact, there is, therefore, no absolute necessity for a chief who is seen as a hero to strive to win his subordinates by adopting a leadership style of democracy and participative management. Many autocratic executives, earnestly disturbed that they cannot seem to feel and act more empathically toward their subordinates, make an effort to do so, but they are simply wasting their time and are fooling no one.

Moreover, it is entirely possible for a chief executive with only a few of the Maverick Executive's qualities to inspire his followers despite his obvious defects. I observed one such executive, the president of a large corporation, who is quite a glamour boy and a demagogue; having a good, intuitive sense of what his employees want and need, he periodically dramatizes the outlook for the company in his "state of the nation" talk, making oblique promises to see to it that his people "are done right by." In effect, he is a con man and a master pitchman. Some of his employees regard him as a charlatan and a mountebank, but nevertheless, though many do not believe him, they still like to hear him. His personal magnetism is enough to inspire a desire to emulate him in a substantial proportion of the workforce.

In much the same way, a chief executive who has previously acquired great status as a national hero or statesman may become a symbolic leader rather than an actual one. (The echoes of Camelot are still reverberating.) He may be seriously deficient in managerial capacities and perhaps shamelessly expedient and manipulative in his private dealings with subordinates. But his public image may symbolize to many employees the embodiment of their goals and ideals, and this engenders the respect and trust they need to feel for him. This is, of course, reinforced by the fact that they see in him what they *want* to see in him. What he actually is and does as an executive is secondary, for it is the *image* that counts, a fact that presidents, kings, and popes have known for centuries.

The real Maverick Executive rarely intends to build a public image and he has little desire to deceive his subordinates with glib promises. Instead, he sincerely and consciously aims to influence them by his charisma, optimism, decisiveness, and toughness. He strives to embody what he thinks most employees would like him to be, and he hopes to reflect their wishes and goals in his behavior. In order to accomplish this, he must be skilled in developing his own "cult of personality." He must convince employees of his inherent strength and his integrity. And he must demonstrate to them, of course, his own competence to do the required job as the leader of the enterprise. He seeks continually for ways to win his employees' admiration, trust, and respect.

An extremely effective means of arousing admiration, respect, and trust in employees was demonstrated by a Maverick Executive's skillful use of employee poll findings. Immediately after the poll was completed he reported the results exactly as they had been given to him and he reviewed with the employees the company's image, warts and all. He then outlined how he proposed to go about correcting conditions that were capable of being changed and explained why not all the conditions could be corrected. Most important, this president took immediate remedial action entirely on his own initiative, not as the result of union or other pressures. To the employees, his actions proved that he was sincere, had their interest at heart, and could be depended on to take remedial action without the imposition of outside pressure.

Most especially, the Maverick Executive must show his interest in the employees as persons and his willingness to help them if necessary. It was said of W. A. "Pat" Paterson, the longtime leader of United Airlines, that when he visited offices and hangars to mingle democratically with the lower ranks, he greeted each person by name and shook his hand. This was not a feat of prodigious memory but a device of conscious symbolic leadership; an aide at Paterson's side unobtrusively gave him each employee's name just before Paterson reached out to shake hands.

All the psychological elements of leadership can be

boiled down to this essential point: the success of a Maverick Executive's leadership lies in the extent to which he can bring his subordinates to identify with him. If they can be induced to do this, they will want to try to emulate him as completely as possible, to look, act, and think like him as best they can. This emulation happens daily with people who enjoy public recognition, our current political, athletic, and theatrical heroes. If the leader is to promote this process of identification, he must to some degree be qualified, rightfully or otherwise, to become a hero.

By stimulating employees to identify with him, the Maverick Executive induces in them the tendency to adopt the values he possesses in dealing with them. And he senses that this process takes place most readily when employees have little actual contact with him. If their dealings with him are too close or personal, they are apt to become disillusioned. In even moderately large companies close contact with the chief executive is unlikely for all except his protégés, for whom such contact will increase their loyalty even though it may somewhat diminish their identification with him.

The more a Maverick Executive succeeds in promoting the process of identification with him, the more he is able to shape the values of his subordinates to accord with his own, and the more uncritical they will be in accepting his orders. When by this process his values have become the ruling values of the enterprise, it is rarely necessary for him to command; it is only necessary for him to indicate the particular course he would recommend. He has then demonstrated the enormous power to be achieved through leadership by *influence*.

This is the most difficult kind of leadership for any executive to achieve. It is not a skill that can be taught in a book or classroom. Nor is it a product of any individual management style; though the Maverick Executive achieves his leadership by managing with his one and only style of benevolent autocracy, this is but one, even a minor, element in his success. At its best, leadership by influence uses many styles of management, but its underlying strength is predicated on a recognition of the followers' dependent needs for a hero or a father figure, together with the flexibility that grows out of a deep understanding of the relations between a leader and the people he leads.

The Maverick Executive simply does not possess this kind of flexible leadership. Rather his leadership is a reflection of the totality of his own personal make-up, his values and goals, and the circumstances—both those he finds himself in and those he makes for himself in his dealings with subordinates. He has neither the insights, nor the diplomacy, nor the flexibility needed to meet the growing demands for more participation in top management that are now coming not only from nonsupervisory employees but from managers as well.

Nevertheless, all the personal elements of his leadership were formed in him well before he took his first job and, since they are essentially unchangeable, they are the best basis for predicting what he will do. Despite his insensitivity to people and his other weaknesses, he is destined to go on exhibiting under all circumstances the kind of benevolent-autocratic leadership by influence that is compatible with everything that he is, believes in, and wants. Judging from the record, his will continue to be an astonishingly successful exhibit of executive performance.